Free Verse

Free Verse

An Essay on Prosody

Charles O. Hartman

Northwestern University Press
Evanston, Illinois

Northwestern University Press
Evanston, Illinois 60208-4210

Copyright © 1980 by Princeton University Press.
First published in 1980 by Princeton University Press, Princeton, N.J.
Northwestern University Press edition published 1996 by arrangement
with Princeton University Press. All rights reserved.

Printed in the United States of America

ISBN 0-8101-1316-3

Library of Congress Cataloging-in-Publication Data

Hartman, Charles O., 1949–
    Free verse : an essay on prosody / Charles O. Hartman.
        p. cm.
    Includes bibliographical references and index.
    ISBN 0-8101-1316-3 (pbk. : alk. paper)
    1. American poetry—20th century—History and
criticism—Theory, etc. 2. Free verse—History and
criticism—Theory, etc. 3. Williams, William Carlos,
1883–1963—Technique. 4. Eliot, T. S. (Thomas Stearns),
1888–1965—Technique. 5. English language—20th
century—Versification. 6. Poetics. I. Title.
PS309.F7H37 1996
811.009—dc20   96-23852
                                               CIP

The paper used in this publication meets the minimum requirements of
the American National Standard for Information Sciences—Permanence
of Paper for Printed Library Materials, ANSI Z39.48-1984.

Contents

Acknowledgments

"Bird-Witted," from *Collected Poems*, copyright 1941 by Marianne Moore, renewed 1969 by Marianne Moore, is reprinted with permission of Macmillan Publishing Co., Inc., and Faber and Faber, Ltd.

"The Dance," from *Collected Later Poems*, copyright 1944 by William Carlos Williams; and "Exercise," "Poem," and excerpts from "Shadows," from *Pictures from Brueghel and Other Poems*, copyright © 1955, 1962 by William Carlos Williams, are reprinted by permission of New Directions.

"The Cupola," from *The Blue Estuaries*, copyright © 1929, 1954, 1968 by Louise Bogan; and "Dream Song #29," from *77 Dream Songs*, copyright © 1959, 1962, 1963, 1964 by John Berryman, are reprinted with the permission of Farrar, Straus & Giroux, Inc.

"Musée des Beaux Arts," from *W. H. Auden: Collected Poems*, ed. Edward Mendelson, Random House, Inc., copyright © 1976; and "Valley Candle," from *The Collected Poems of Wallace Stevens*, Alfred A. Knopf, Inc., copyright © 1968, are reprinted by permission of the publishers.

"Church Going" is reprinted from Philip Larkin, *The Less Deceived*, 1952, by permission of The Marvell Press, England.

Excerpts from "Burnt Norton" are reprinted from T. S. Eliot, *Collected Poems 1909-1962*, by permission of Harcourt Brace Jovanovich, Inc., and Faber and Faber, Ltd.; copyright 1943 by T. S. Eliot; copyright 1971 by Esme Valerie Eliot.

"The Ground-Mist," from *O Taste and See*, copyright © 1964 by Denise Levertov Goodman, is reprinted by permission of New Directions.

Seven lines of "Summer School," from *The Life Beside This One*, copyright © 1975 by John N. Morris, are used by permission of Atheneum Publishers.

Portions of "Self-Portrait in a Convex Mirror," from

Self-Portrait in a Convex Mirror, copyright © 1975 by John Ashbery, are reprinted by permission of Viking Penguin, Inc.

Four lines from "Chard Whitlow," by Henry Reed, are reprinted from his book *A Map of Verona* by permission of Jonathan Cape, Ltd.

Preface

A study of free verse must deal with its origins and development, and therefore with the history of poetry in the twentieth century. Yet my purpose here has been less historical than theoretical. I wanted to understand, and explain my understanding as best I could, what free verse is and why it works, as well as how it is related to other kinds of verse. The examples—the analyses of poems on which my reader's conviction must finally rest—were chosen for the clarity with which they demonstrate the ways of nonmetrical verse, and sometimes for their representative nature. I have avoided using poems that did not excite me. But the examples do not by any means constitute an anthology of all the best modern free verse; nor will the reader find, among their authors, all the greatest poets of our century.

My interest in the questions explored here grew out of my own experience in writing poetry, both metrical and nonmetrical. It was my father, Carl F. Hartman, who originally set me on the track of several ideas presented in these chapters; my first thanks are due to him. When the book began to take shape, I had the splendid assistance of Jarvis Thurston, Howard Nemerov, Donald Finkel, and above all Naomi Lebowitz, at Washington University. Later, a Fellowship from the National Endowment for the Humanities to the School of Criticism and Theory at the University of California, Irvine, helped me to understand what I was doing in relation to some present intellectual concerns; Barbara Herrnstein Smith, especially, confirmed the influence she had already exerted through her book, *Poetic Closure*.

My thanks go also to Meredith Steinbach for her editorial acumen. Hazard Adams kindly read the manuscript and commented in helpful detail. Finally, I want to express my gratitude to Dr. Catherine Wallace, of Northwestern University, where the book took final shape; without her minute, comprehensive, and sympathetic criticism, what follows would have been far less than it is.

Seattle, Washington

Free Verse

The Prehistory of Free Verse

In 1908 the world was in order: Edward VII occupied his mother's throne; with the usual minor exceptions, peace reigned; Darwin's theory was well on its way to universal acceptance, and it was easy to read into his *Origin of Species* a doctrine of gradual, inevitable progress. People thought in terms of progress, slow but sure, not only in politics and economics but also in their whole culture (or Culture), particularly the arts. The Great War was still six years away.

That year T. S. Omond wrote a short article on the subject of verse for a widely read intellectual journal, *Living Age*. At least, we can assume it was Omond: the author signs himself "T.S.O.," the subject is generally prosody, and those are the initials of one of the great traditional prosodists. In the article, he poses an innocent question: "It is not uninteresting to ask what determines the length of verse-lines" (81, 119).[1] Omond observed that the length of lines readers were willing to accept, and poets were therefore willing to try, had gradually increased until "Tennyson ventured at last on nine beats." This progress might be sustained, but Omond dared to doubt that it "can be considerably prolonged without substantial other modification" (81, 122).

Other modification was about to arrive. But even after it did, the traditional "science of prosody" would continue to work itself toward perfection. Omond's own study, *English Metrists*, had been published in its first version a year before his article. He had taken up a position straddling the gap between Sidney Lanier and George Saintsbury. Saintsbury's monumental three-volume *History of English Prosody* would not be finished until 1910 (publication had begun in 1906), but it codified laws of verse laid down over five hundred years. English metrical theory had begun awkwardly, in the six-teenth century, by taking from Latin (originally Greek) the terminology developed for quantitative meter. This imported system never completely left the English scene, and in 1880 Lanier's *Science of English Verse* dressed it in a new finery bor-rowed from music and set it up as a challenge to the accepted view. Saintsbury implicitly supported the mainstream ("ac-centualist") position, condemning Lanier bitterly along the way. Omond was more or less ground up between these stones.

Thus a basic disagreement divided the foremost scientists of prosody. "Even at the point of the highest development of English prosody as a science (say about 1900)," Karl Shapiro remarks, "two scholars of equal prominence could debate whether the line, 'The mountain of the gods, the unappeasa-ble gods,' was metrical, one insisting that it was a 'palpable Alexandrine' and the other questioning whether it was verse at all" (93, 77-78). Yet the fundamental agreement that under-lay these differences was even more striking, in light of what happened shortly afterward. Verse was composed of metrical feet, made either out of long and short syllables or accented and unaccented ones. The dominant foot in a poem gave the meter its name. Perhaps other kinds might replace it more or less often. Prosodists debated this point with some heat, though in retrospect trisyllabic substitution seems one angel more or less on the pin's head. The debates were the refine-ments of experts. Elsewhere, prosody was well enough un-derstood to be taught to children in school.

In this generally confident prosodic atmosphere, poets were taking advantage of all the elaborations the system allowed. Swinburne was especially fond of metrical experiments (Al-caïcs, double sestinas, and the like), though Tennyson had probably tried everything that needed to be tried and suc-ceeded brilliantly with all that could succeed. But with so or-derly a range of possible permutations, it seemed a shame not to give each its chance. Everyone, poets and theorists alike, was less willing to move outside the established English system. Of course there were other meters; the French counted only syllables, Coleridge had revived the Old English method of counting only stresses (Hopkins's work was still unknown), and a scholar might point out that the Chinese used patterns of tones or pitches. But those would require a different science of prosody. Except for the perennial wistful hankering after quantity (Swinburne's Alcaics and Sapphics, later Bridges's hexameters), no one cared to abandon so rich a prosodic tradition as that which ran from Chaucer through Shakespeare up to the Edwardian present. Some peculiar poems had been produced by Whitman; but even the American poets were more typically represented by Whittier and Longfellow. Prosodists who thought about Whitman at all agreed with his own characterization: His was a "barbaric yawp." So when Omond asked about the length of lines, his question assumed narrow limits. He wondered only how many feet could be strung together. What he meant by "other modification," he himself probably did not know.

Also in 1908, Ezra Pound's first book was published. It was printed in Venice; it offered no prosodic innovations. But after four years—by 1912: the year when Saintsbury's *History of Prose Rhythm* affirmed the principles of his earlier work; the year when the same journal that had printed Omond's article first called Gustav Krupp a war criminal—Pound would formulate Imagism. He would command the young poet who wanted to be an "Imagiste," the modern thing to be, "to compose in the sequence of the musical phrase, not in sequence of a metronome" (87, 3). Taken by itself, the dictum is ambiguous and vague. Lanier had espoused musical rhythm in poetry, Walter Pater had said decades before that all art should aspire to the condition of music, and surely no poet had ever consciously venerated the metronome. But in the context of the time, Pound was coming down for *vers libre*.

Vers libre: free verse. The phrase itself was a contradiction in terms. Theorists of prosody were quick to point out the absurdity of the idea. Poets who were both attached to the experiment and willing (often eager) to wage war in the periodicals, together with a few editorial types and other hangers-on, published their side of the argument in whatever journals were willing to admit them. There were not many, at first. What is interesting about the whole controversy is the passion, even fanaticism, with which it was pursued. Any magazine concerned in any way with poetry took one side or the other. (The *Dial*, which printed articles on both sides, changed hands in the middle of the fray.) The fight went on for at least ten years, not abated by the War that broke at nearly the same time. The connection is not frivolous. In many respects the issues in the two conflicts were perceived as similar, however different their scale.

If "free verse" were to be admitted as verse at all, everything that had been achieved in the study of prosody would have to be rethought. Verse itself was defined, and still is in many dictionaries, as "metrical composition." As late as 1931, a writer on the poet's craft could still insist that "the word *verse* originally meant and still means a single metric line divided into feet. As commonly used it has come to mean metric composition as distinguished from prose" (56, 4). But the issue was larger still. If the definition of verse were in question, so would be the nature of poetry, with which it was habitually confused. And poetry was the pinnacle of civilized achievement, part of "what we fought the war for" against the barbarian Hun. The metrical system handed down from generation to generation of poets and refined theoretically by generation after generation of prosodists was the very heart of poetry. The prosodic theorists were defending civilization itself. Hence the almost apoplectic attacks on the New Poets: "These men are the Reds of literature [1921]; they would reverse or destroy all the recognized rules and standards upon which literature is founded" (24, 551). At the time, this was not even hyperbole, but metonymy. Meter equals verse, equals poetry, equals culture, equals civilization.

Thus traditional prosodists, faced with the appalling fact of free verse, were forced back to their original assumptions, many of which they had never before needed to think through. Prior even to the definition of verse was the realization that "metrical composition" depends on conventions. The prosodic system was a structure of conventions supporting, requiring, and implying each other. The very possibility of reading poetry (that is, verse; that is, metrical verse) depended on everyone, both poet and reader, subscribing to the same conventions. This assumption was fundamentally correct, though we will want to refine it. But many writers displayed an unfortunate tendency—still common—to confuse "convention" with "propriety." This reinforced, and perhaps derived from, the whole alliance of poetry with the established social order. When this confusion was carried far enough, it became possible to talk about "free verse" and "free love" in the same tone.

Obviously everyone did not subscribe to all these equations. But on one thing both sides agreed: The "science" of prosody was at stake. If free verse could be ousted or put down, prosody would be saved. If not, it would fall. And that is what happened. Free verse turned out to be something that poets would continue to write, though not exclusively, and readers would read. It became one of the species included by the word *poetry*. (The inclusions of such a word are matters of convention. Conventions change.) And prosody—as a system, as a theory, as an object of study—almost ceased to exist. Books were still written, of course, though fewer. Most of them ignored everything that had happened since the turn of the century. A few came to terms with the earlier manifestations of free verse. Saintsbury tolerantly discussed Blake and Ossian (1910), and Gay Wilson Allen gave the first clear account of Whitman's methods in his *American Prosody* (1935). Prosody is now largely in the hands of linguists seeking structural formulae for meter; it is not taught in the schools. The few exceptional writers on prosody (such as Harvey Gross) have lacked the community of interest that encourages a scholar. After brief and half-hearted attempts by a handful of writers in the magazines during those first years of con-

troversy, few have tried seriously to study English prosody in
any way that could include poetry written after 1912.

How could they? According to the definitions established
by the science of prosody, free verse was prose by default.
This was the most common charge against it—we will exam-
ine it in detail. Free verse was irrelevant to prosody, and
prosody to it. The break with the prosodic past seemed as
great as the First World War's destruction of historical certain-
ties and modern literature's denial of all that had come before.
Yet no such break is absolute. For decades now it has been one
business of critics to demonstrate not only the ways in which
modern literature is new but the ways in which it continues
literary tradition. Though we tend to regard our century as
unique, we know that so have those of previous centuries re-
garded their own times. We have come to understand the
Great War as an event like any other large event (a Greater
one helped): It made enormous differences, but it grew out of
the past and left many things as they were.

The same balance can be achieved in our view of prosody.
We have lived long enough with free verse and metrical verse
to see them on more even terms. The vitriol has mostly
evaporated. Unfettered by the need either to attack or defend
free verse, wanting only to understand it; believing that there
are no wholly new things but only new combinations and
uses of old things; we can ask again the question that pros-
odists during their last debate could not pose clearly: What are
the essentials of prosody?

I begin by asking how free verse is possible and how it works.
This question occupies about half the book. Chapter One of-
fers, as its title says, some definitions—a pedestrian but neces-
sary start. Chapter Two outlines the positions that prosody
took after free verse began, and the theories I want to oppose.
The third chapter returns to the question of what conventions
remain to guide poet and reader once meter is gone, and how
those conventions can work prosodically. Chapter Four
analyzes the most common free-verse prosody, showing how

it controls meaning in poems. This is the analytic center of the book. The last chapters turn to broader and more elusive problems having to do with the different kinds of free verse and the poet's relation to his poem. Chapter Five discusses the modern development of "organic form" as the guiding rhetoric of verse; it concentrates on poems by William Carlos Williams. In the sixth chapter most of the examples come from T. S. Eliot, whose free verse is less clearly divorced from meter than Williams's, but related to the same principles examined in the previous chapter. Next I ask about the connection between free verse and the poetry written in it, especially at first, and this question leads once more to the historical position of free verse. In the last chapter, I look at more contemporary verse and its prosody, in order to see where these developments may be leading.

Chapter One

Some Definitions

To begin with the name: Does "free verse" mean anything at all? Is it, as its opponents charged, an oxymoron like "foolish wisdom"? "No *vers* is *libre*," said T. S. Eliot, "for the man who wants to do a good job." Can any meanings of the two words plausibly coexist?

The odd phrase symbolizes the confusions that threw the study of prosody into such disarray. "Free verse" was one of two names given, first by detractors and later by the poets themselves, to nonmetrical poems. It competed with the French it translated, *vers libre*. In 1920 Amy Lowell, while expatiating on Modern Poetry, remarked that "our English substitute for the French term is thoroughly misleading" (73, 141). One is tempted to agree. But she mistook the source of confusion: "The French word *vers*," she noted, "does not mean 'verse' but line." This merely shifts the ambiguity to English; as an opponent pointed out, not only *vers* but " 'verse' actually means line if we use our terms accurately" (57, 392-93).

Our language contributed to imprecisions like Lowell's. The confusions intensified by the name and fact of free verse were already implicit in the whole subject. They are still manifest in the very words we use, so that it becomes difficult to "use our terms accurately." "Verse," for instance, has taken on three meanings. In historical and logical order, they are: a line of poetry, a group of lines (a stanza or strophe), and the form or process whose usual paraphrase, "metrical composition," begs the questions posed by free verse. In fact, ambiguities becloud both parts of the phrase; "free" is yet more obscure. It will be simplest to begin by looking more carefully at "verse."

"Verse" is sometimes used interchangeably with "poetry." Exactly or not, one can speak of "poetry" in relation to an immense range of human activities and experiences, not all of which involve language. If I say "poetry in motion," people will have at least a vague sense of what I am talking about. That sort of sprawl makes a word comfortable, but nearly useless for analysis. "Poetry" seems impossible to define rigorously and permanently. "Verse" is bad enough; but it has the advantage of referring clearly to the form of a linguistic expression, not its content or value. It is one of two such forms, established by convention, the other being prose. An opposition between prose and poetry, though common enough, is also commonly rejected.[1] "Prose-poems" exist. "Prose-verse" contradicts itself; the words oppose each other exactly. Even so, distinguishing them is one of those problems that attract critics by providing inexhaustible grist. Northrop Frye's essay, "Verse and Prose" (88, 885-90), which grinds both terms very finely, shows how complex the question can become.

Yet to make a clear and simple distinction, we need only remember what Howard Nemerov calls "the hard-nosed definition laid down by Jeremy Bentham, that when the lines run all the way to the right margin it is prose; when this fails to happen, it is [verse]" (80, 129). *Verse is language in lines.* This distinguishes it from prose. (There is a logical connection, it seems, between the original meaning of "verse" and the more general one.) This is not a really satisfying distinction, as it stands, but it is the only one that works absolutely. The fact that we can tell verse from prose on sight, with very few errors—Nemerov (80, 126-35) describes an amusing and instructive one, interpreting a pair of addresses as a lyric—indicates that the basic perceptual difference must be very simple. Only lineation fits the requirements.

That this distinction is more powerful than it seems will be my theme in later chapters. The point here is that, understandably, it would have satisfied few students of prosody in 1912. Their emphasis on metrical organization as the defining trait of verse had its own analytic virtues; with modification,

it is still useful. To go beyond traditional definitions profitably, we must account for them, use what we can from them,
and provide for the functions they served. An idea of prosody
that accounted only for free verse, or that assumed its centrality, would be as false and otiose as those that presuppose
meter.

I said a moment ago that poetry could not be rigorously
and permanently defined. To search out an exclusive definition—one that will not only include everything that can or
should be called poetry but will exclude everything else—is to
seek the chimaera or the true shape of Proteus. But one can
construct any number of inclusive definitions, which cover all
kinds of poetry and too much else besides. Most of these beg
the question in one way or another, by depending on words
like *aesthetic* or by mere vagueness. I want to suggest one,
however, that will provide a reasonable basis for a theory of
prosody: *A poem is the language of an act of attention.* But whose
act of attention is the poem? The poet surely has to perform
one in writing it; and as readers we often hypothesize or project such an act as the motivation of the poem, which in this
sense "represents" it. But the act of attention is also our own
as readers. The poem is its cue, its control, and in this sense its
"opportunity." Standing alone between poet and reader, the
poem serves as the matrix for both their acts of attention.

The definition still needs narrowing; it will not distinguish
poetry from prose fiction or a telegram. Rigorous distinctions
of this kind may well be impossible. But we can at least learn
more about poetry by considering its relation to space and
time. This question is old and troublesome. Certainly both
space and time are involved, but it seems to me that the spatial
characteristics of poetry have always been secondary. Our
poetic conventions derive from a time when poetry was not
only aural but oral. There would seem to be reasons for retaining this fiction. Some philosophical and theoretical critics
now interest themselves in *écriture*, in books as books and not
as records of speech. If this idea should gain ascendancy over
the way we read, the spatial element in poetry might take on a

greater importance. Some hints of this have already appeared, as in the poems of Cummings or in more recent "concrete poetry." Also, written verse always involves some admixture of spatial organization. The shape on the page of metered stanzas creates a presumption of order; this allows flexibilities that would otherwise court anarchy. (A comparison with songs, such as I have made elsewhere [45; 47], dramatizes this point.) Nevertheless, for the present we continue to think of language, and thus verse, as a temporal medium.

This brings me to the term a book on prosody most needs to define: *The prosody of a poem is the poet's method of controlling the reader's temporal experience of the poem, especially his attention to that experience.* But how can the poet control the reader's experience? How does the reader know what to pay attention to, among the many linguistic events the poem comprises? The prosody, to function as a prosody, must be shared. This implies a communication between the poet and the reader; but the only communication would seem to be just those facts (marks on a page) whose characteristics are in question. Yet there is also an indirect communication. The poet can count on the reader to share, not only the direct experience of the marks, but the context of conventions within which they become a set of words (the conventions of a language), and beyond that a passage of verse (the convention of lineation), and beyond that a poem with a particular prosody. As traditional theorists partly recognized, prosody depends essentially on conventions.

To create and control attention requires organization—or at least that is the most obvious way to do it. This may tempt us to distinguish poetry or verse from prose on the grounds that prose is less highly organized. But it has often been shown that any mode of organization found in any poem (except lineation) will also occur in some passage of prose—usually in many, though rhyme, for instance, had a short and relatively disastrous career in English prose. Organization disappoints two hopes prosodists have entertained. It is not a measure that will absolutely distinguish prose from verse; only lineation

can do that. Nor can it distinguish prose from poetry; proba-
bly nothing will. But it does provide a set of tools for the
analysis of prosody.

What I have already said about the temporality of poems
suggests that prosodic organization is rhythmic. *Rhythm, in
poetry, is the temporal distribution of the elements of language.* Ac-
cording to this definition, all language unavoidably has
rhythm. But it follows from my earlier definitions that poetry
makes us especially aware of rhythm. As the Gestalt psychol-
ogists have been demonstrating since the Great War, organi-
zation or structure lies, to an important extent, in the eye of
the beholder. The more attention one pays to rhythm, the
more profoundly one is likely to perceive it as organized.
Whatever the "facts"—and they may be impossible to deter-
mine in isolation from our experience of them—rhythm in
poetry generally *seems* more highly organized than in other
uses of language. This suggests a form of my definition of
prosody that approximates and includes the traditional one: It
is *the system of rhythmic organization that governs the construction
and reading of a poem.*

"Organization" implies elements to be organized, and pro-
sodic organization will employ the elements of speech: (1)
timbre (in recurrences such as alliteration, assonance, and
rhyme); (2) duration (which, when applied as it commonly is
to syllables, is called quantity); (3) pitch or intonation; (4) in-
tensity or volume (these two being distinguishable acousti-
cally but not psychologically, and so not prosodically); and
(5) boundary. The first four are commonly accepted as the
elements of all language.[2] This is not so true of the fifth,
which may help to clarify some aspects of my definition of
prosody.

Boundary is demonstrably necessary as a prosodic element.
Without it, as W. K. Wimsatt and Monroe Beardsley point
out in one of the best modern treatments of meter, the charac-
teristics of standard prosodic forms grow hazy: "To have
verses or lines, you have to have certain broader structural
features, notably the endings. Milton's line is not only a visual

or typographical fact on the page, but a fact of the language. If you try to cut up his pentameters into tetrameters, for example, you find yourself ending in the middle of words or on weak words like 'on' or 'the' " (108, 591). Ending on "on" or "the" would destroy Milton's prosody; it is acceptable, even normal, in the prosodies favored by William Carlos Williams or Robert Creeley. Milton's line, in short, is determined by more specific conventions than the phrase "a fact of the language" would suggest. But in any case, endings make meanings. The effects of lineation (to be discussed in Chapter Three) depend on line boundary. Furthermore, at least within Milton's prosody, the length of words and the distribution of their junctures become significant rhythmic elements. As Wimsatt and Beardsley observe, the inherent flexibility of iambic pentameter "combines further with the number and length of the words involved in a line to produce contours of tension so special as perhaps better not translated into any other kind of meaning but simply regarded as shapes of energy" (108, 597). Such "shapes of energy" are among the effects of prosody. A simple example is the trick known to any careful writer of iambic verse: A two-syllable word crossing a foot boundary will tend to speed the line up, while one that coincides with the foot will slow it down. "Foot boundary"—like lineation—is obviously not a fundamental element of all language, but it has become essential to some prosodies, as lines are to all.

Yet this presents a puzzle. Some historical linguists, thinking how language originates in speech, might claim that word boundary—so lately introduced into typography—is not really part of language. And syllable boundary is often imperceptible to the eye. Perhaps one or the other, but not both, could be organized rhythmically in verse, depending on whether verse speaks to the eye or the ear. But prosody obviates disputes about the precise linguistic status of various kinds of boundary. We recognize both word boundary and syllable boundary because we have learned our language both by reading and by listening, just as we recognize foot bound-

ary when we have learned to scan metrical verse. As the
example of foot boundary demonstrates, these elements act in
our understanding of verse as conventions rather than as sim-
ple acoustical or spatial facts.

As Wimsatt and Beardsley remark, "The main thing to ob-
serve about the principles of relative stress and counted sylla-
bles is that by means of these you can explain the necessary
things about English syllable-stress verse" (108, 593). "The
necessary things" means the information a reader must share
with the poet. This is not to deny that other elements have
rhythmic effects in a passage of verse, but the poet will choose
one, or a combination, to dominate his prosody. The choice
will be determined partly by his language. Each language
trains the ears of its speakers to attend more to some charac-
teristics of sound than to others. Thus in each poetic tradition
one or two rhythmic elements are likely to dominate and de-
termine the conventional prosody, though the poet may be
able to use others. (The difficulty of doing so is clear in the
attempts of English poets to import quantitative organiza-
tions from the languages that gave English its *theoretical* pro-
sodic tradition.) In Chinese, for instance, words are monosyl-
labic, so word boundary and syllable boundary reinforce each
other. Pitch distinctions (the four "tones") are also clearly
marked and semantically important. Chinese prosody tends
to combine these, distributing set patterns of tones over set
numbers of words. In French, a language with minimal ac-
cent, the traditional prosody organizes syllables. On the other
hand, Anglo-Saxon had prominent accents, closely linked
with meaning, and their rhythmic organization constituted
Anglo-Saxon prosody. English, influenced by French, de-
scended from Anglo-Saxon. Latin contributed a foot-based
theory, which requires two prosodic elements (in the case of
Latin, syllabic quantity and boundary). It is not surprising
that English prosodies have depended upon both syllable
boundary and accent.

I should pause to say something about accent as a prosodic

element.[3] It is not one of the elements of speech as I listed them earlier. Rather, accent is compounded of intensity, pitch, and to some extent duration. It frequently implies something about timbre as well. (Stress often changes timbre—"evil," "establish"—though not always: "defense.") Furthermore, accent is sometimes governed by particular linguistic conventions (as in polysyllables), and sometimes depends on context. The pitch factor in accent takes its own place in a complicated system of "pitch contours" indigenous to the language (84). The placement of accent also involves the meaning of the words, which it both determines (is "permit" a noun or a verb?) and is determined by.[4] (One can read "I don't want it" in at least three ways. If we encounter it on a page, only by considering its contexts—prosodic and other —do we know where to put the accent.) Because accent is so powerful semantically, and so evident to the ear, English favors it for prosodic organization, along with syllable boundary.

Besides elements, organization requires a mode, a *how* as well as a *what*. The linguistic elements a poet organizes prosodically are largely chosen for him by the conventions of his language; but each poetic tradition also dictates, by establishing more-specific conventions of verse, what he does with these elements. In almost every case, this traditional mode of organization is or depends on a numerical rule. When this is the case, we call the prosody metrical. *A meter is a prosody whose mode of organization is numerical.* Obviously such a rule only works prosodically when shared by poet and reader; a convention must endorse it. But conventions determine the possible constituents—both mode and element—of any prosody, and this will not distinguish clearly between metrical and nonmetrical prosodies. I have already mentioned some examples of meters: The French Alexandrine is twelve syllables long; the Anglo-Saxon line comprises (usually) four accents; English accentual-syllabics count both syllables and accents. We must return to this, our tradition's dominant prosody, but

first I want to exemplify these general principles with two
meters whose unfamiliarity helps them avoid some confu-
sions.

Rhopalic verse is a peculiar form that illustrates the work-
ings of meter fairly simply. Its prosody organizes both word
and syllable boundary by a numerical rule: each word in a line
exceeds the last by one syllable. The *Princeton Encyclopedia of
Poetry and Poetics* gives only one example; it is in Greek, and is
complicated by the simultaneous presence of a quantitative
hexameter:

ὦ μάκαρ 'Ατρείδη, μοιρηγενές ὀλβιόδαιμον
(*Iliad* 3.182)

One can invent an English example, though it is hard to sus-
tain a long passage:

The circus imitates metaphysics' circularities.

The oddness of this form resides in only two characteris-
tics—its unusual reliance on word boundary and its simplic-
ity.

It is worth asking whether such a line would not have
seemed anarchic to a poet or critic of the English metrical tra-
dition. Would he not have taken it for a line of "free verse"?
Of course it has a meter, and free verse by definition does not.
But a closer look dissolves the hard and fast distinction. In
some sense any verse form is "free" with respect to any other,
as the rhopalic line I invented is free if measured by the rules
of iambic pentameter. It is "free" until its prosody is discov-
ered. The reader easily discovers the prosody of a poem that
belongs to his own tradition. But when the prosodic conven-
tions on which a poem depends are alien to his experience, the
poem will puzzle or completely mystify him.

Thus, in a poem like Marianne Moore's "Bird-Witted," the
first stanza feels and looks and sounds like free verse, or even
like a random lineation of discourse—discourse whose gen-
erally prosaic (though elaborate) diction and syntax seem to
underscore the arbitrariness of the lineation. Yet glancing

down the page at the similar shapes of the second and later stanzas, the reader who is aware of French poetry can deduce that Moore has extrapolated from strict syllabic meter, organizing it in stanzas rather than in lines. Syllabic meter is not a dominant prosody in English. But for six stanzas the poem repeats, and thus makes deliberate, the random-looking pattern of its beginning, "just [58] syllables per stanza, flawlessly divided, 9, 8, 6, 4, 7, 3, 6, 4, 7, 4" (62, 163). Hugh Kenner, whose description this is, takes this "flawless division" as a sign of the poem's integrity, an integrity of form that imitates or acknowledges or substantiates the integrity of the bird which the poem takes as its subject and whose actions make up its content.

Our language does not maintain rigid strictness in determining syllable boundary. Sometimes one has to consult a word's place in the pattern to decide its pronunciation. "Cruel" in the eighth line of the last stanza needs two syllables to give "cruel wings, the" its quota of four; but the beginning of the second stanza and the second line of the fifth compress "toward" to a monosyllable. Nevertheless, we marvel at the tidiness of the scheme; and all the more when, with Kenner's adroit help, we see the feats Moore simultaneously performs with her rhymes, imitating various aspects of the singing of the birds, including (in the third stanza) their silence.

This conviction of order is not really shaken when we discover three consecutive lines that will not conform, whatever the Procrustean reader does to them. The fourth stanza remembers the sweetness of the birds' song at mating time (78d, 106). After preening, a wing

    is closed again. What delightful note
      with rapid unexpected flute-
    sounds leaping from the throat
      of the astute
    grown bird, comes back to one from
    the remote

> unenergetic sun-
>   lit air before
> the brood was here? How harsh
> the bird's voice has become.
>
> A piebald cat observing them,
>   is slowly creeping toward the trim
> trio on the tree-stem

—the three fledglings the mother must protect. The penultimate line of the fourth stanza ("the brood was here? How harsh") contains six syllables rather than seven; the next also has six, instead of four; and the first line of the next stanza is eight rather than nine syllables long.

These anomalies in the prosody seem like mistakes only for a moment. Their place in the poem, where its plot reaches a climax, reveals their function. Standing against the strict syllabic pattern, they introduce the same sort of discord as the cat, disordering the song of the mother bird. We think at first that her voice has become "harsh" simply from the toil of feeding the fledglings, detailed in the three previous stanzas. Not until the beginning of the fifth stanza do we see the more urgent, immediate reason. The cat is not mentioned until the last of the anomalous (discordant) lines; like the observer in the poem, we do not see the cat until after we have heard of it, heard its effect on the bird's song. This is an impressive act of mimesis, the prosody itself (or a discontinuity within it—the distinction depends on which form of the definition one uses) serving as a sign of the experience that the poem enacts.[5] It exemplifies the power of a metrical prosody to generate meaning by variation on a regular, strict pattern.

Moore wrote her syllabic poems after the advent of free verse. I doubt that she would have written them before. The possibility of doing without meter entirely had led poets to think more carefully about meter itself. Besides its effects on the continued writing of accentual-syllabics, this encouraged the use of meters until then unusual or unknown in English. This could extend even to Louis Zukofsky's attempt, described by Kenner, at a system that "governs the distribution of 'n' and 'r' sounds according to the formula for a conic section. Who would think of counting the n's and r's? Yet the poet's 'intention to have it fluoresce as it were in the light of seven centuries of interrelated thought' has chosen that rigorous and hidden way of impressing itself upon the language" (60, 189). Yet all I have said about the importance of convention should explain why such a meter—and it is undeniably a meter and thus, strictly speaking, "a prosody"—does not really function as a prosody. As with "boundary," we need to distinguish between objective facts ("the distribution of 'n' and 'r' sounds") and information that conventions have made available to the poet and reader. A wholly new ("hidden") meter is not a prosody as far as the reader is concerned, because he does not share the secret. The difficulty of turning new principles of rhythmic organization into prosodies was the general problem faced by the inventors of free verse.

I want to give as a final example of meter the one we as English readers know best, the accentual-syllabic prosody that is still with us. Growing out of merged but competing systems from French, Anglo-Saxon, and Latin, it is as complex in its basic principles as any ever invented (100). This creates much of the richness of possibility that half a millennium has far from exhausted.

As its origin and name declare, our meter depends on two rules: counting accents and syllable boundaries. (Further organizations are often added—rhymed stanzas, the complexities of villanelle and sestina, and so on.) At its most rigid, the pattern demands that every line contain (for example) ten syllables, and five accents or stresses in the even positions. But this double rule contributes to the form's flexibility. Because the number of accents is set, the number of syllables can vary, within limits; because the number of syllables is set, the accents can vary in position and strength, again within limits. Poets may take greater or less advantage of this flexibility. The pentameter exhibits historical cycles, receding from and developing toward strict observance. In Sidney and Pope it flowers into regularity; their expressive variations gain power from formal restraint. The meter of Wyatt and Donne permits broader gestures. Like them, Browning plays freely with the pentameter's accents, while Hopkins quite disrupts the syllabic norm. Although these cycles will not really account for free verse, the poems of Eliot and others sometimes seem like logical extensions of this irregularity. Before returning to free verse, however, I want to use this meter to explore a last defining question about prosody.

Crude as it is, scansion—the simple diagrammatic indication of stresses and slacks—tells us all we have to know about a poem's meter. The meter itself, like the scansion, is an abstraction. It is the rule to which a line more or less conforms, and not the line itself. It is not rhythm, but a pattern imposed on rhythm. Not only the unmetered elements of language (such as timbre and quantity), but also the actual instances of the metered elements, the particular stresses and syllables of the line, continue in some sense to occupy the more general area of rhythm. "Rhythm is not metre," Owen Barfield remarks. "It is not another name for metre, but something far subtler. Rhythm is variable about its underlying regularity, whereas metre is invariable" (12, 793). Meter *is* the "underlying regularity" played against by rhythm. These two maintain a continual and fructifying tension, like any actuality and the abstractions that shape it.

This distinction need not be a matter of metrical variations, substituted feet. Two lines that scan as perfectly regular metrically inevitably vary in rhythm:[6]

The curfew tolls the knell of parting day . . .

I do not think that they will sing to me . . .

One could scan these lines differently only by indicating the caesura, which is very weak in both and belongs only marginally to meter anyway (though it is important rhythmically). Yet Gray has linked the adjacent accents "tolls" and "knell" with consonance for a primarily onomatopoeic effect, while Eliot joins the separated, balanced accents "think" and "sing" with assonance to suggest a conceptual opposition. (The thoughtless sensuality of the mermaids' song will not tempt Prufrock out of the constant "visions and revisions" that are his thinking.) While Gray coordinates his accents with the important words, five nodes of significance, Eliot diffuses significance among his "ten low words" without much differentiating stress, words carefully chosen for their plainness and their refusal to assume individual emphasis. All these differences, which the meter will not disclose when we scan it, are differences in rhythm.

Several early writers on "the New Poetry," working from a metrical tradition yet failing to maintain this basic distinction, fell into serious error. James Oppenheim, trying to clear a territory for what he obscurely called "tune," claimed that "Yes, my dear's like a pretty rose" has "the same rhythm" as "O my luve's like a red, red rose"—an absurdity traceable to too narrow an idea of rhythm (82, 70). Conrad Aiken, writing in 1918 on "The Function of Rhythm," seems to have made the same mistake. He could only call free verse "verse without rhythm"—as if that were possible—because what he meant by "rhythm" was actually meter (2, 418). H. E. Warner, a firm enemy of free verse, could say that "certainly rhythm is the one essential element of poetry, but rhythm, as applicable to poetry, and metre are identical, so far as I can see, with time in music" (103, 386). This "musical fallacy" will concern us later; but it is the assumption that "rhythm . . . and metre are identical" which allows Warner to equate both with "time in music." Most important, this is the assumption that betrayed one critic after another into thinking of free verse as a kind of prose. Warner goes on to show how the same initial confusion of rhythm with meter fosters this misconception: "there is a sort of rhythm in the most prosaic prose, and as the feeling which strives to clothe itself in language becomes intense, the language will become more rhythmic; that is, it will more and more take on the form of

the traditional meters" (102, 91). Such passages represent a
disaster of terminology and definition.[7]

Yet though one must maintain the distinction to establish a
clear theory of meter, in practice it dissolves. The distinction
itself implies that the primary prosodic rule of a poem—a me-
ter, for instance—is never solely responsible for the poem's
rhythmic organization. By bringing strict order to one
rhythmic element, a numerical rule focuses the reader's atten-
tion, not just on that element, but on rhythm as a whole. In
my rhopalic line, recurrences of sound—"circus," "cir-
cularities"; "imitates," "metaphysics"—spring to the eye and
ear as soon as one's attention is captured by the prosodic rule.
The same effect attends any prosody, metrical or not. Al-
though in a narrow sense the prosody of my line is rhopalic,
my broader definition of "prosody" would include all the acts
of rhythmic attention the line demands and embodies—
rhythm as well as meter, when the latter exists.

I have gone the long way round to get to free verse. But I
think several points about meter have emerged that bring
other prosodies into perspective. If "free verse" simply meant
verse whose principles of organization differ from those of
English accentual-syllabic meter—as I suggested incidentally
and as many early opponents of free verse assumed—then it
would include Moore's syllabics and Zukofsky's mathe-
matics. But most of what we call free verse does not resemble
this. Nor does "free" imply the kind of license that so hor-
rified its opponents. Free verse, like all verse, is prosodically
ordered and not aimless; this is my basic assumption.
Rhythm, to function as meaning, must be prosodically or-
dered, and some convention must endorse that order if the
poet is not to fall into Zukofsky's trap. To see how free verse
actually works, we will have to ask what conventions remain
after metrical rules are abandoned. The line of argument I
have followed throughout this chapter already allows us to
understand at least the theoretical possibility of free verse.
"Free" is properly a synonym for "nonmetrical," and it fol-
lows that *the prosody of free verse is rhythmic organization by other*

than numerical modes. How many such modes are imaginable would be hard to say; but two examples should clarify the issue.

I have implied that multiple rhythmic patterns—not all of them metrical and perhaps none—can coexist within a given passage of verse. These multiple patterns may reinforce each other, or they may stand in conflict. In the latter case, we can generally expect to perceive conflict on one level as meaning on another, as any paradox ultimately disproves (but does not deny) itself. This kind of significant conflict I will call *counterpoint*, though "tension" might do almost as well. "Tension" has the advantage of its physical metaphor, and the mixed blessing of a psychological implication. But I prefer "counterpoint" because this seems to me one of the few areas in which really illuminating parallels can be drawn between music and poetry without serious danger of confusion. Furthermore, "tension" emphasizes the origin of meaning in conflict, while "counterpoint" stresses the meaning into which conflict resolves. It directs attention to the end of analysis rather than to analysis as an end in itself. How counterpoint works as a prosody demands a chapter to itself; but obviously it represents a mode of organization that is not numerical.[8]

A second mode is symmetry. Free verse rarely uses a symmetrical prosody in a primary way. It would give a poem too tedious a stability. But when such elements as accent function at all prosodically in free verse (as they usually do, because of the nature of the language), they often adopt a symmetry that seems to arise out of the actual line, unlike an imposed numerical quota. An example of the symmetrical arrangement of accent, from a poem I will discuss later, is Williams's line,

Maybe it's his wife.

The symmetry is elaborated in the next line,

The car is an official car,

where the repetition of a word reinforces the pattern of stress.
These patterns do not constitute the poem's prosody, but they
are important rhythmic details within more general prosodic
systems.

Though symmetry rarely occurs as a pervasive principle, it
is quite feasible within a traditional metrical scheme. Any
headless line of iambic verse is technically symmetrical, as a
pentameter by Wyatt shows:

  Í haˇve séen thˇem gén̆tle, táme ănd méek.

Yet because we recognize that the poem from which this line
comes belongs to an iambic metrical tradition, we are unlikely
to perceive the symmetry as such. In some cases, it can seem
that metrical and symmetrical organizations stand in inverse
relation, the rise of the latter destroying the former and mov-
ing the line into free verse. Consider this more complex
example:

  Shivering in their beds in November's wind.

Here, ordinary metrical compensations keep control. The first
foot is inverted, the fourth is an anapestic substitution, and the
first "in" is metrically promoted to (relative) stress. We read
the line as iambic pentameter. But change the form of the
verb and something different begins to happen:

  Shiver in their beds in November's wind.

A reader sensitive to both the accentual and syllabic compo-
nents of English meter will notice that, although the line can
conceivably be regularized, a pattern is generated within the
line itself that is nonmetrical and, if not narrowly "symmetri-
cal," more like that than like the recurrences of meter. The
best conventional scansion would come close enough to
breaking the iambic norm so that the natural speech rhythm
of the words takes over instead: / x x x / x x / x /.
In this four-stress line the slack syllables suffer a constant de-
crease between accents. This pattern is "numerical" in one

sense; but it is not imposed. We perceive it as a pattern not because we have seen it before, but in spite of the fact that we have not. As a pattern, it does not come from any conventional system (though it is the conventions of English that make us attend to accent and syllable in the first place); therefore we see it as arising from the words themselves.

This internally generated pattern creates its own implication—paring away superfluities for the sake of increasing solidity and finality—which differs from the feeling of balance precariously achieved that the rhythm would suggest in a metrical context. In both cases rhythm functions as meaning, but the meanings are different. The contexts make the difference, but the line disrupts iambic norms radically enough to make a metrical context unlikely. A sonnet containing the line would need to domesticate the line by preparing for an initial defective foot, though the scansion is unsatisfactory in other ways, or bury the line in a longer syntactical sweep, or settle on the present-participle version. In a free-verse poem, however—a poem not bound by the same expectations as iambic pentameter—the internal symmetry of "Shiver in their beds in November's wind" would give the line a pleasing, if grim, neatness that contradicts the air of anarchy it assumes when read metrically. The line could end a free-verse poem, but not a sonnet.

Ultimately, "free verse" is "free" only in a special sense. Poems are written in verse so that the rhythms of language can contribute to the whole meaning of the poem; and it is prosody of one kind or another that turns rhythm into meaning. Impulses toward individuality and originality and novelty were among the motives for developing alternatives to meter. Seeking liberation, the early modernist poets managed to open up new prosodic possibilities. But prosodies, as organizations, are limitations. Some writers needed to believe that "every man's free verse is different" (97, 156). Clearly this cannot be true. Prosody depends on conventions. Eliminating those of meter merely throws the poet back on those that define verse and govern language in general.

What is important about free verse is the new insight it gives into the whole question of prosody in *any* verse. It neither aids nor distracts the reader with an abstract pattern he can transfer in detail from poem to poem and codify in a formally closed, quasi-mathematical system that bears only incidentally on the experience of poetry. Because the reader cannot pretend to account for its rhythms in abstract isolation, free verse confronts him directly with the complex relation of rhythm to meaning. It forces him back into the poem; and that is where he has always belonged. This is the reminder about all poetry that free verse offers to the poet, to the reader, and finally to the student of prosody.

Chapter Two

Accentualism, Isochrony, and the Musical Fallacy

"The New Poetry" faced a serious charge: Free verse was "formless." Somehow its defenders had to demonstrate that it was an honest alternative to the dominant metrical tradition, less like a defective mammal than a bird. Yet they were hampered by assumptions of their own, which the same tradition had shaped. It suggested that the most obvious way to give free verse a place beside accentual-syllabic verse was by discovering or inventing for it an equally abstract system, equally independent of actual poems. They must find, many concluded, a new meter for the new poetry.

These anxieties sprang, as we have seen, from false premises. Both the defenders and their antagonists misunderstood "free." Old confusions rose up to haunt them, and one especially led them into elaborate error. Mary Hall Leonard exemplified it in saying that Coleridge, Blake and Chatterton, "instead of the regular iambics of the Popian era, . . . adopted an irregular iamb-anapestic form of rhythm which laid strong emphasis on the accented syllables, the number of weak syllables that were swept along with these being considerably varied, and this became known as 'free' or 'accentual' verse" (68, 15). This equation stood behind the most thorough and widespread attempt to rationalize free verse. The whole complex of ideas it generated deserves attention. To understand both the reasoning and its flaws, we need to review some earlier stages in the practice and theory of English prosody.

THE TRADITION IN PRACTICE

Accentual meter seems natural in the heavily stressed Teutonic languages. As the Anglo-Saxon prosody (along

with alliteration), it begot our modern English system. Like
its offspring, it is a meter, depending on a numerical organiza-
tion; but it counts only the accents in a line, not the syllables.
The two meters require different handling. Anglo-Saxon
verse, written in half-lines of two stresses each, rarely allows
three-stress lines, and never five. Accentual meter has to be
relatively strict to exist at all. (Only the concomitant struc-
tural alliteration—rarely duplicated in modern imitations—
gives Anglo-Saxon prosody what freedom it has.) Although
any series of English words has accents, this does not make it
an accentual line. For the accents to constitute a meter, they
have to be measured. At least on a clear average their number
must remain constant. All single-element meters share this
limitation, which makes them more brittle than complex
prosodies like those of Latin and modern English. The flexible
accentual-syllabic meter can bend in two directions. If its ac-
centual rules are loosened the line approaches a syllabic norm,
and vice versa.

   It may be the historical primacy of accentual meter that has
repeatedly tempted English poets to relax their lines in the
second way, by allowing syllable counts to vary beyond met-
rical limits. Coleridge's "Christabel" provides a clear exam-
ple:

　　'Tis the middle of night by the castle clock,

　　And the owls have awakened the crowing cock;

　　Tu—whit!—Tu—whoo!

　　And hark, again! the crowing cock,

　　How drowsily it crew.

Coleridge's Preface throws an amusing light on this crude
verse. He celebrates his prosody as one using "a new princi-

ple," then goes on to describe the oldest meter in the language.

Yet Coleridge also felt obliged to insist that "this occasional variation in number of syllables is not introduced wantonly, or for the mere ends of convenience, but in correspondence with some transition in the nature of the imagery or passion" (27, 25). Once convention has included a rhythmic element in the dominant meter, the poet cannot lightly ignore it. Once accentual-syllabic meter had been established, the purely accentual line seemed like a relaxation, and the poet had to justify it in relation to conventional principles. Defenders of free verse could see a moral here.

But the case of Gerard Manley Hopkins points a different moral, concerning the danger that such justifications may confuse the conventions to which they appeal. Most of Hopkins's poems employ accentual meter, though their odd density of diction sometimes obscures the principle (52):

> I cáught this mórning mórning's mínion, kíng-
>   dom of dáylight's dáuphin, dápple-dawn-drawn
>
>   Fálcon, in his ríding
>
>   Of the rólling lével underneáth him steady áir, and
>   stríding
>
>   Hígh there, how he rúng upon the réin of a wímpling
>   wíng

"The Windhover" begins with an iambic pentameter whose regularity helps him establish the five beats of later lines. He leaves the reader careful prosodic clues: using hyphens to subsume "dapple-dawn-drawn" into one accentual unit; marking adjacent stresses in the otherwise ambiguous line,

>   No wonder of it: shéer plód makes plough down sillion;

and allowing pervasive alliterations to recall his Anglo-Saxon model.

To these poems in relatively clear accentual meter, however, Hopkins appended a profusion of explanations, replete with his own enchanting terminology of "sprung rhythm," "outrides," and "rove-over lines." His theories fight out a place for his poems within the traditional foot-based system. Yet though his arguments all derive from that system, they war peculiarly against it. He declares that all poetic rhythms are falling rhythms, and confines the possible feet to the single stress, trochee, dactyl, and first paeon (15, 419). If these statements are irrelevant to simple accentual meter, neither do they make sense within an accentual-syllabic system based on the supremacy of the iamb.

Hopkins the theorist remains puzzling until one realizes that accentual meter is not the only prosody Mary Hall Leonard might have described as laying "strong emphasis on the accented syllables, the number of weak syllables that [are] swept along with these being considerably varied." We hear another one in nursery rhymes, chants, game songs, work songs, and ballads. This prosody originates in music. It depends on a beat or pulse—not counting the accents, but equalizing the time between them: isochrony, it is called. Confusingly, in music this principle is called "meter" (108, 589). But though it is a prosody—it controls the audience's temporal experience more directly than most—it is not a meter in the poetic sense. It organizes rhythm not numerically but temporally. Just as more or fewer events (syllables or notes) can crowd between the stresses, so the place of a stress itself can be left empty. The "trimeters" in a ballad stanza— though the term is not really appropriate—are filled out to the same length as the "tetrameters" by a silence, a rest. The possibility of definite rests distinguishes isochrony from any other prosody.

Such verse is not built up of feet in the usual sense, but of measures, as in music. The stress that defines and creates each measure does so by marking its beginning. This explains

Hopkins's insistence that only "falling" feet—those that begin with a stress—occur in his system. (Hopkins's poems also show that measures cut across and even replace lines when they can. If all feet are falling, the unstressed beginning of a line must belong to the line preceding. This indifference to lineation allies isochrony more closely with music than verse.) The fact remains that Hopkins badly muddles together accentual meter, isochronous prosody, and a foot system appropriate to neither. But the third was forced upon him by prosodic tradition, and the first two are easily confused. Though isochronous prosody only marginally belongs to poetry—its natural home is in song—the lines of distinction are not always easy to draw (45; 47). The two- or four-measure melodic phrases of traditional songs *tend* to enforce a regular number of accents per line, if only in broad stanzaic patterns. Though isochrony is not numerical, it closely resembles accentual meter; and in some cases, such as ballads, one can discriminate between them only arbitrarily.

To put it another way: Once words give up the rhythmic support of music, the number of isochronous units is easily regularized, and the temporal prosody becomes one of two meters. In a stress-oriented language, it becomes accentual meter. In a language whose temporal details remain more fixed, such as Greek or Latin, isochrony develops into quantitative meter. The surprising connection between these two meters will come up again when I turn to the theoretical tradition.

First, I want to summarize the possibilities that these considerations suggest. The viability of accentual meter is demonstrated not only by all of Anglo-Saxon verse and by such experimenters as Coleridge and Hopkins, but also by contemporary poets like John N. Morris, to whose "Summer School" this brief quotation does not do justice (79):

Gradually in the evening

Under the trees

That are outlásting ús,

We disappéar. The móthers,

The móthers are cálling

The chíldren of óthers,

. Cálling them hóme.

What especially interests me about the prosody of this poem
is the way Morris, while maintaining the accentual meter, al-
lows the shadow of an iambic trimeter to play against it. The
tradition again proves too powerful to ignore—though it can
be domesticated by contrapuntal use. But Morris's poem also
shows, like Marianne Moore's syllabics, how the new pro-
sodic freedom of our century has encouraged poets to try
previously unusual meters.

The quantitative meters, on the other hand, though at-
tempted by poets as far apart and as skillful as Campion and
Bridges, continue to resist importation into English. Quan-
tity, considered simply as the duration of syllables, is a
rhythmic element in any verse, often an important one. But
because English recognizes no established, conventional rules
for determining the quantity of a syllable, metrical organiza-
tions based on it risk inaudibility. As Wimsatt and Beardsley
put it, "long and short syllables are not found in the English
dictionary. . . . Quantity is a dimension where you cannot
make mistakes in pronouncing English. And where you can-
not make mistakes, you cannot be right, as opposed to
wrong. It follows that in such a dimension a writer in English
cannot create a public pattern. The English language will not
permit a quantitative meter" (108, 588-89).[1]

The final alternative, the isochrony of accents, is a difficult
prosody to maintain in poetry. I have noted some reasons.
The main one can be indicated by asking how the poet can

make his reader understand that his prosody is isochronous. If the poem measures accents, isochrony becomes a superfluous principle; in any other case, why should the reader suspect its presence? One solution to this problem characterizes the late poetry of Williams. His own accounts approach those of Hopkins in obscurity. But evidence collected by Emma Kafalenos, in a dissertation called *Possibilities of Isochrony*, shows that Williams meant his three-line stanzas to be read so that each line occupies the same amount of time as the others.[2] Lineation marks the isochronous units. The prosody works, for two reasons. First, it builds on the convention of line division, essential to and recognized in all verse. Second, Williams became sufficiently well-known so that through letters and essays he could establish single-handedly the convention that all lines take the same time—though only for his own poems. His very success points up some of the interlocked problems of publicity and convention that plagued free verse at its inception. It also hints that prosodic practice sometimes depends on published theory as much as theory on practice— and so suggests the rhetorical character of free verse that will concern us in Chapter Five.

The Prosodists' Tradition

Though accentual and isochronous organizations have their own light to cast on modern prosody, I am concerned with them here mainly as they have served some writers' attempts to rationalize all free verse in metrical terms. The preceding discussion should help to place these attempts within an old debate about the whole nature of English verse. Two dissenting views have recurred, a sort of far right and far left of metrical politics.

On one side is the group sometimes called "nativist." These writers see the Old English meter not as merely cropping up from time to time in a Coleridge or a Hopkins, but as abiding continually in English verse. For them it stands behind and informs the iambic pentameter, showing through the façade of French and Latin accretions like the structure of a Saxon church. Northrop Frye aligns himself with this group: "The iambic pentameter provides a field of syncopation in which stress and metre can to some extent neutralize one another. If we read many iambic pentameters 'naturally,' giving the important words the heavy accent that they do have in spoken English, the old four-stress line stands out in clear relief against its metrical background" (39, 251). The tetrameter, which dominated English verse briefly before the pentameter took over, probably does owe nearly as much to memories of the four-stress line as to the French octosyllable. And in most pentameters the five metrical accents do not have equal force. But neither do the four accents of an Anglo-Saxon line; all linguistic stress, in speech as well as verse, is relative stress.[3] If the prosodist thinks of the tension between rhythm and meter—which is what Frye is talking about—as an opposition between the abstract pattern imposed by meter and the actual movement of speech in the line, he can go on to hypothesize that the Anglo-Saxon measure still represents the genius of our tongue and often asserts itself as we read a pentameter. But often ("many iambic pentameters") is not always, and it is not enough to constitute a metrical principle. The pentameter did replace the tetrameter, and the nativist theory makes it hard to understand why. The accentual line may recur as one part of the rhythm in pentameter lines, but it does not help in describing their meter. Where is one to put the four accents in "The curfew tolls the knell of parting day"? Trying to account for the line metrically, one is forced back to the principle enunciated by Wimsatt and Beardsley: "The main thing to observe about the principles of relative stress and counted syllables is that by means of these you can explain the necessary things about English syllable-stress verse" (108, 593). Stress by itself is inadequate. As a way of accounting for English verse as a whole, accentualism collapses.

Over the centuries, far more prosodists have rallied behind the opposite standard, favoring the importation of quantitative meters into English. They have wanted to complete the invasion that extreme nativists try to turn back. Before free verse got under way, advocates of quantity found their champion in Sidney Lanier (*The Science of English Verse,* 1880), the great rival of George Saintsbury. (Saintsbury was not a nativist, either; he held to the middle of the road. Though he was sometimes called an "accentualist," this meant only that he frowned on too much emphasis on quantity. Unlike a true accentualist, he analyzed English lines in terms of feet; but for him they were composed of stressed and unstressed, not long and short, syllables.) Lanier's theories directly influenced several of the later writers on free verse.

A word about scansion may clarify what I have to say about Lanier. To scan accentual verse, one can only mark the accents, as I did earlier in the poems of Coleridge, Hopkins, and Morris. To construct feet around these accents would be inappropriate—Hopkins's theories amount to an attempt at this. When a meter is based directly on time, however, quite elaborate systems become both possible and informative. They are as essentially musical as the meter itself. Latin macrons and breves could be translated without loss into quarter notes and half notes or any other diagrammatic representation of time values. Here lies the main burden English took on in adopting the Latin system. Our dominant meter stands at some distance from musical principles; yet the system brings with it assumptions that apply only to a time-based prosody. Even Saintsbury succumbed to the confusion. Karl Shapiro, speaking of Saintsbury's idea of "equivalance," which seeks to explain how trisyllabic feet can appear in iambic verse, points out that what Saintsbury "knew and tried so hard *not* to say was that equivalence is the temporal or quantitative element in English versification which equalizes unequal accentual elements by varying the *time* of feet, whether in the ear or in the recitation of the verse. This, however, is a principle of music, and the mention of music was heresy and anathema to Saintsbury" (93, 81). One solution would have been to realize—as Shapiro seems not to do—that the questions raised by the concept of "equivalence" have only a secondary bearing on English verse, and to drop or revise the concept. The other would have been to embrace the musical, temporal, quantitative theory of Lanier.

Lanier failed to understand that quantity is not a sufficiently definite element in the English language to support a meter. The flaw becomes obvious as soon as one looks at his scansions. Beginning from the assumption of a quantitative prosody, he rightly chooses a musical notation; but here is the logical result:

To be or not to be—that is the ques-tion.

Harvey Gross's comment seems definitive: "The musical scansion of Sidney Lanier's *The Science of English Verse,* praised by T. S. Omond, Harriet Monroe, and others, remains a dismaying example of a theory ridden sadly beyond the limits of good sense. A 'scansion' which gives this sort of thing is worse than useless; it scatters sand in the eyes and pours wax in the ears" (43, 7).

Behind the absurdity lurks an error that vitiates much writing on prosody. One might call it the "performative fallacy." As Wimsatt and Beardsley point out, "There is, of course, a sense in which the reading of the poem is primary; this is what the poem is *for.* But there is another and equally important sense in which the poem is not to be identified with any particular performance of it, or any set of such performances" (108, 587). How could Lanier have arrived at his scansion, prosodic pioneer that he was? He began with the principle of isochronous measures, each containing an accent. If he had marked the accents and left it at that, I could only repeat that he invoked an inadequate principle. But the deceptive accuracy of musical notation tempted him to aim at greater precision: stress doubles a syllable's length, syntactical breaks and line breaks correspond to specific durations of silence, and so on. He sought more exactness of prosodic analysis than any scansion can provide. The conventions embodied by an English dictionary offered no help; he could only turn to performance. He carefully read the line aloud and notated, carefully, what his ear gathered from his voice. But this means that his scansion represents not the meter but part of the rhythm; one reader's temporal experience, not the principles that control it.[4]

A moment ago I opposed the quantitative view to that of the nativists. But earlier I showed that they do not entirely contradict each other, since both confuse accentual-syllabic meter with prosodies based on time. Thus, within a page after Frye's statement supporting the nativist position, he gives a set of musical scansions. Finally, both dissenting accounts of English meter break down precisely because they deny the common view. Both claim to demonstrate "what really happens" in an iambic pentameter line. Prosody is not a fact that "really happens" in this sense, and this is especially clear when we are considering a long-established meter. If generations of poets have thought they were writing accentual-syllabic meter, not accentual or quantitative, and generations of readers have agreed, they were right by definition. To deny this is to pretend that verse exhibits factual characteristics independent of convention, and that these facts outweigh conventions in a reader's experience. This leads to a basic misunderstanding of prosody, which employs a system of conventions to provide part of the context within which reading becomes possible.

PROSODISTS OF FREE VERSE

Among modern prosodists, Harriet Monroe (whose administrative services to verse as founder and editor of *Poetry* deserve gratitude) merely followed Lanier in trying to explain accentual-syllabic meter in quantitative terms (77). But Amy Lowell took Lanier's theory a step further. By reducing his quantitative system to the isochrony on which it was founded, she tried to account for free verse. In some ways this

enterprise offered more hope. No common view need be de-
nied, except the negative one that free verse lacked all
rhythmic order. She could not run afoul of convention in
quite the same way as Lanier and Monroe.

She began in 1917 by declaring that "the 'beat' of poetry, its
musical quality, is exactly that which differentiates it from
prose, and it is this musical quality which bears in it the stress
of emotion without which no true poetry can exist" (71, 46).
A year later she had encountered Dr. William Morrison Pat-
terson, and embarked on scientific discoveries. Their collab-
oration constituted a striking attempt to apply technology to
questions of prosody. Lowell and Dr. Patterson experimented
with photographic representations of sound, measuring in
tenths of a second the time "between chief accents." They
found that a certain interval consistently reappeared in her
reading of any given poem. H. D.'s "Oread," for instance,
had an interval of "return" of 13/10 second. The form of that
poem, Lowell explained, "is non-syllabic, in that the chief ac-
cents come after a greater or lesser number of syllables. The
units conform in time—allowing for the slight acceleration
and retardation of the unitary pulse, guided by an artistic
instinct—but not in syllabic quantity [that is, the number of
syllables]" (72, 53). Is the "artistic instinct" her own, or the
poet's? In any case, her allowance for variation, though prom-
ising, did not prevent her from reading "several poems to a
metronome. The reading did not, in every case, exactly fol-
low the metronomic swing, but the variance was so slight as
to be accounted for by the natural acceleration and retardation
of the artistic impulse" (72, 54). Obviously these experiments
say more about Lowell as a reader than about the poems she
read; but I want to follow to her conclusion.

From the experiments, Lowell drew a comparison between
metrical verse and free verse (which she related to music by
calling it "cadenced"): "Cadenced verse is non-syllabic, and
in that sense resembles music far more than the old metrical
verse ever did. As music varies the numbers of notes in a bar
by splitting them up into smaller time valuations, so cadenced

verse may vary the number of its syllables within the duration of its time-units to any extent desired" (73, 141). With Patterson's help she had stumbled upon the connection between accentual and quantitative verse, in the isochronous, musical implications of both. However confused her explanations, she clearly saw free verse as splitting up the accentual-syllabic meter and replacing syllable counting with isochrony. The result must closely resemble accentual meter, to which I will return, but her theory contributes its own special errors.

To begin with, Lowell's proof that free verse is isochronous depends on a peculiarly modern version of the performative fallacy. She believed that Patterson's photographs and measurements would yield facts about the verse that could explain its prosody. To have anything to photograph, she must perform the poem. It is not just the idiosyncracy of a single reader that invalidates the result. Other experimenters—authors of an article, "Perception and English Poetic Meter"—had a group of people read poems in unison (19). The record of this reading showed an isochronous beat. It could hardly have done otherwise. How else are people to read a poem in unison? Game songs and work songs use an isochronous prosody for the same reason. The proof, as circular as that of Lowell's metronome, proves nothing.

After Patterson had obtained his photograph, he could measure the intervals exactly. But it was a spurious precision, like Lanier's. What was he really measuring? Harvey Gross explains the logical flaw in asking recording devices to tell us the truth about prosody:

> As a formal element in poetry, meter is an immediate perceptual given: we have the demonstrably audible and measurable facts of stress, quantity, pause, and number. But, we insist, the sounds and silences of meter are not perceptual entities as such; we do not respond to metrical texture as we do to fine silk or highly polished wood. The acoustic arrangements of meter are images of time shaped and

> charged by human feeling. The machines currently
> used in prosodic analysis show what happens in an
> arbitrary temporal sequence. The oscillograph
> knows nothing of *durée*, of time grasped and under-
> stood by human awareness. . . . The results of the
> machine are a tautology because no machine under-
> stands the uniquely human import of symbolic
> structures; the machine returns a set of symbols still
> requiring human interpretation [43, 19].

So, one might add, does the ear or eye of a listener or reader.
The "human interpretation" derives from a system of pro-
sodic conventions.

Finally, the isochrony Lowell discovered cannot function as
a prosody, not because it has no part in English speech—the
central difficulty of quantitative meter—but because it has too
common a part. Every utterance in the language tends to
equalize the intervals between accents. Kenneth Pike, the lin-
guistic researcher, has shown that the time-lapse between any
two primary stresses tends to be the same irrespective of the
number of syllables and the junctures between them (84).
Lowell and Patterson would have found their isochronous
intervals of "return" if they had used prose rather than free
verse, or metered verse as in the group-reading experiment.
Failing to distinguish between free verse and metrical verse,
Lowell's theory can hardly account for the former.

If isochrony proves inadequate, can we look to accentual
meter for a general principle of free verse? Several writers
have tried. Some poets whose verse employs the meter see
other modern verse as doing the same. Yvor Winters some-
times oversteps the line between his own and others' poems:

> I do not wish to claim that the [free-verse] poets of
> whom I write . . . had my system of scansion in
> mind when writing their poems. Probably none of
> them had it. What I wish to claim is this: that the re-
> ally good free verse of the movement can be scanned
> in this way, and that the nature of our language and

the difficulties of abandoning the old forms led in-
evitably to this system, though frequently by way of
a good deal of uncertain experimenting [110, 115].

Winters's first sentence should make us wonder whether he is
really speaking of prosody, which can hardly work uncon-
sciously. John Gould Fletcher, whose "Rational Explanation
of Vers Libre" (37) is a deeply confused explanation of ac-
centual meter oddly mixed with quantity, was another who
proceeded inductively from his own poems to free verse in
general.

That we cannot rely on this inductive argument is best
shown by the different example of Harvey Gross, who, in his
invaluable *Sound and Form in Modern Poetry*, sometimes finds
accentual prosody where I cannot discover it. For the begin-
ning of *The Waste Land* he prefers (to an accentual-syllabic
scansion he has suggested) this accentual or "strong-stress"
version (43, 38):

April is the cruellest month, ‖ breeding

Lilacs out of the dead land, ‖ mixing

Memory [and] desire, ‖ stirring

Dull roots ‖ with spring rain.

Gross's rhythmic analysis provides important insights; but his
scansion does not indicate an accentual meter. The third line
has only three stresses. In other lines one could easily argue
for or against various accents: Why stress "Dull," and not
"out"? In an accentual poem, these questions could be flatly
answered, because once the metrical rule has determined the
number of accents in a line, it is never too difficult to locate
them, even in poems as complex as Hopkins's. But here, what
demonstrates that such a meter is present except the claim to
have scanned it—a scansion which must itself depend on the

presence of the meter? With no convention to establish that
meter as the poem's prosody, the line merely has accents, like
any series of English words. I will return to Eliot in a later
chapter. But already one can see that hypothesizing an accen-
tual meter will not explain his verse; nor will it account for all
free verse. To call all verse accentual that does not count syl-
lables is no solution.

The theories of isochrony and accentualism belong to the
same enterprise and share the same flaws. In both cases, if the
elements the prosody requires can be shown to exist, they can
be discovered equally well in any bit of speech. Prosody re-
quires more. The inevitable presence of a rhythmic element
does not demonstrate the poet's *control* of temporal experi-
ence. By the arguments of these various writers, all English
verse—perhaps all English—is accentual and isochronous.
The arguments make distinctions impossible; they defeat
their own purpose.

Out of all this comes only one working nonmetrical pros-
ody: Williams's isochrony of line. As I have already said, it
works because Williams managed to set up his own conven-
tion for his poems (built on the fundamental convention of
lineation and the pervasive fact of isochrony). To a smaller ex-
tent, Yvor Winters could do the same, and even John Gould
Fletcher. Each poet's system collapses when it attempts to
colonize all free verse. Consider this final example, from the
end of the *Princeton Encyclopedia of Poetry*'s article, "Free
Verse": "In f[ree] v[erse] . . . the bracket of the customary
foot has been expanded so that more syllables, words, or
phrases can be admitted into its confines. The new unit thus
created may be called the 'variable foot,' a term and a concept
already accepted widely as a means of bringing the warring
elements of freedom and discipline together" (88, 289). The
circle in which the term "variable foot" is accepted, or even
understood, is in fact a very narrow one, comprising the most
diligent scholars and loyal followers of William Carlos Wil-
liams. So this statement in the authoritative *Encyclopedia* puz-
zles us, until we notice that the contributor signs himself
"W.C.W."

Chapter Three

Free Verse and Prose

If isochrony and accentualism will not account for free verse, then the charge of formlessness remains to be answered. Other verse gives us, through shared conventions, a metrical organization that contributes intricately to the meaning of the poem. This justifies what we might otherwise find annoying. Verse imposes a visual inconvenience, after all; it is harder to read than prose. Of free verse, one might be tempted to ask, Why not print it as prose? Furthermore, many free-verse poems are so slight, so brief and apparently trivial in what they say, as to compound the annoyance. After printing the thing as prose, why bother to read it? Some systematic answer must unite these two questions. It emerges when one asks a third: Why is poetry usually written in verse?

PROSE AND VERSE

My question recalls those with which I began, about relations among prose and verse and poetry.[1] In my first chapter I argued that verse and prose differ in kind. But writers during the great free-verse controversy more commonly assumed that the distinction involves only differences in degree. In their articles one can trace various forms of this belief, from vague suppositions to sophisticated principles.

To those who sought room for new forms, the old opposition between prose and poetry, the latter defined narrowly as metrical verse, began to seem too confining. Why not instead take poetry or verse as one end, and prose as the other, of a continuous spectrum? For F. S. Flint, "The one merges into the other; there is no boundary line between them," and one can discriminate only among the generic uses to which they are put (38).

For Conrad Aiken, free verse was "this form which lies half-way between" (2, 418). Henry B. Fuller called free verse "neither verse, on the one hand, nor prose, on the other. Between black and white are shades of gray; between high tones and low, serviceable octaves intervene; between noon and midnight there is a borderland of dusk or of dawn. Free verse balances on the fence between poetry and prose, and dips beak or tail toward either at will" (41, 516). Amy Lowell advocated the same theory, and wished "to establish a division in the spectrum of word-values, and to show how the extreme of prose at one end changes to the extreme of poetry at the other, through the grades of 'metrical prose' and *'vers libre'* " (74, 213). Lowell's busy scrutiny fostered the inevitable development, a proliferation of intermediate possibilities. Her collaboration with Dr. Patterson, which I discussed in the last chapter, produced not only their theory of isochrony, but seven divisions "in the spectrum of word-values": metrical verse, "unitary verse," "polyphonic prose," "spaced prose," "fluid prose," "mosaics," and "blends" (72, 55).

Distinctions were often couched in comparative terms, as matters of more and less: "We use [free verse] because we must, because it is more real than the conventional metres and . . . is directed by an intenser rhythmical ardor than prose" (97, 154). So says Edward Storer, whom I quoted earlier as claiming that "every man's free verse is different." (Does that insistence on individuality depend on some latent idea of a spectrum?) He goes on to declare that between "rhythmical prose" and free verse "there is perhaps no arbitrary difference, but there certainly is a difference of degree." The same difference obtains between prose and free verse—the midpoint—as between free and metered verse. John Gould Fletcher, the accentualist, takes the same tack: "A piece of verse must have a certain form and rhythm, and this form and rhythm must be more rounded, more heightened, more apparent to both eye and ear, than the form and the rhythm of prose"(37, 12).

All these theorists and theories tended to converge on the word *cadence*. The convergence was more lexical than semantic, since the word came to mean whatever a writer liked. Some claimed that verse or poetry has it, while prose does not; others assumed that both manifest it but in different degrees; still others, or the same writers on other occasions, insisted that "prose cadence" and "verse cadence" differ in kind. For some it was synonymous with free verse itself, and opposed to meter. The word was never really defined. Although it was Amy Lowell's solution to the taxonomic problems that intrigued her, her paraphrase clarifies little: "By 'cadence' in poetry, we mean a rhythmic curve, containing one or more stressed accents, and corresponding roughly to the necessity of breathing" (73, 141). How does it operate in verse? Does it correspond to the line? What makes it effective or appropriate? How does one recognize it? What is the material of the "curve"? Richard Aldington combined "cadence" with comparatives, saying that in free verse "the cadence is more rapid and more marked" than in prose (3, 351). Lowell herself sometimes jumbled differences in kind and in degree almost inextricably: "Now, there is a difference between the cadence of vers libre and the cadence of oratory. Lincoln's Gettysburg address is not vers libre, it is rhythmical prose. At the prose end of cadence is rhythmical prose; at the verse end is vers libre. The difference is in the kind of cadence" (65, 8). Mary Hall Leonard, though she adopted the word, despaired of any analytical profit from this approach: "That the cadence which belongs to polished prose may have varying degrees is obvious. But as to its division into *kinds* of cadence, no writer, not even Amy Lowell herself, has ever pointed out any basis on which *kinds* of cadence can be distinguished" (68, 20).

Lowell's interest in kinds of cadence implies a certain uneasiness at the idea that prose and poetry might loosely flow into one another. Like others, she seems to have longed half-consciously for a firmer distinction. George Saintsbury had provided one in 1912: "As the essence of verse-metre is its identity (at least in equivalence) and recurrence, so the essence of prose-rhythm lies in variety and divergence" (91, 450). Verse is defined by the presence of "verse-metre," which in turn depends on repeated rhythms. Saintsbury himself could afford to be casually generous toward oddities he turned up like the "prose-verse" of Ossian, Blake and Whitman: "An exceedingly hasty or untrained judgment may feel inclined to say, 'Oh! this is not verse, so it must be prose.'. . .[But] it is not safe to call it prose . . . something more than prose . . . has been aimed at . . . it has (in measure differing no doubt according to the taste of the appreciator) been achieved" (91, 471). He went on to note, however, that "whether Prosody will receive it as a subject is out of our concern" in a book on prose rhythm (91, 472). His earlier remarks on such forms in the *History of English Prosody* are no less cagey (92, III, 91–46). But those interested in free verse could not avoid the question so easily, and phrases like "something more than prose" did not help. The term "verse-metre" encumbered their efforts by invoking the old equations. Perhaps one could simply change it to "verse-rhythm," opposing it to "prose-rhythm"? But when poets abandoned meter, they discarded the systematic duplication of rhythmic units ("identity and recurrence") on which Saintsbury's distinction depends. Robert Bridges, in his "Paper on Free Verse," tried to apply the principle of recurrence to a form which the identifiably repeated feet of traditional meter no longer set off from prose. He suggested that "what is verse to some hearers is prose to others; and since there is no short speech-rhythm in prose which might not be used as a metrical rhythm or a part of some metrical system, the only difference would seem to be that in prose the rhythms were not evident or repeated; if repeated you would come to expect them" (21, 649). Perhaps an "intermediate form" like free verse "may combine some of the advantages of both systems: it might possess in some measure the freedom of prose and the expectancy of verse." But in the terms Bridges adopted this seems contradictory. And indeed he concluded about free verse that "we should be prepared to find that in discarding the distinctions which perfected the old types, it lost their most forcible characteristics." Distinguishing verse from prose on the grounds of repeated rhythms, one ends by proving free verse unworkable.

It appeared that Saintsbury's distinction could be employed only by discriminating verse- and prose-rhythms more absolutely, seeking an inherent difference among the single units. In "The Borderline of Prose," T. S. Eliot approached the problem this way. "Both verse and prose," he maintained, "still conceal unexplored possibilities, but whatever one writes must be definitely and by inner necessity either one or the other" (32, 159). Taking as his example one of Aldington's prose-poems (Eliot does not accept the term), he submits that

> if this is read as prose, it is found jerky and fatiguing, because there is a verse rhythm in it; and that, if read as verse, it will be found worrying, because of the presence of prose rhythms. . . . I conclude that the only absolute distinction to be drawn is that poetry is written in verse, and prose is written in prose; or, in other words, that there is prose rhythm and verse rhythm. And any other essential difference is still to seek [32, 158].

As late as 1963, in the course of a diatribe against free verse that accuses Eliot as the arch-offender, A. D. Hope implicitly agrees with his enemy's assumptions. Free verse arises from the mistaken belief that

> poetry can be improved or its range extended by breaking down the traditional structure of English verse or replacing its rhythms by those of prose. The English metre depends upon collocation of metrical and prose rhythms and from this comes its elasticity, its richness of texture and its endless possibilities of variety within a simple pattern. So-called free verse sacrifices all this by trying, and trying in vain, to make the prose rhythms do all the work [51].

Yet despite Eliot's and Hope's declarations, neither one attempts to define "verse-rhythm." (Hope implies a definition, but one that confounds rhythm and meter in a way the dangers of which I have described.) The attempt would surely have been futile. As Bridges said, "there is no short speech-rhythm in prose which might not be used" in metrical verse. Just so, "cadence" could be said to belong to one as well as the other, and no one ever found "any basis on which *kinds* of cadence can be distinguished." Even if one were to take these theories as intuitively correct, none of them provides much help for analysis or reading. They are too vague to explain the way a piece of verse actually works, or even to distinguish it from prose. Even those that begin with clear demarcations between verse and prose end, when applied to free verse, with doubtful comparatives.

Among the early writers on free verse, only Owen Barfield seems to have understood all this as a mistake. In an apparently unnoticed article, "Poetry, Verse and Prose," he identified a "confusion of thought" whose source "lies in the modern tendency to regard concentration on hybrids or borderline cases as a means of clearing up typical differences. . . . Whereas in point of fact these borderline cases are the most likely ones of all to confuse our minds, inducing us to ask the wrong kind of questions, and to forget what we are inquiring for in the ardour of inquiry" (12, 794). Lowell and others asked what lies between prose and poetry. Such a question generates its own answers, as when Lowell searched out the spectrum's seven hues. These burgeoning subdivisions entangle the prosodist in fruitless taxonomic disputes.

In this welter of conflicting theories, one begins to wonder what caused so much confusion. Many writers rebelled against the old equation of poetry with meter, because it allowed no place for free verse. But most saw their task as the careful delineation of territories within what remained a single state. Before free verse, the only recognized secession was the "prose-poem," which still left verse to be identified with meter. (This may explain why Eliot disliked the term, though he used the form.) On the other hand, few prosodists heeded the warning that prose-poems offered against equating poetry with verse. In several of the passages I have quoted, it is impossible to tell which is being opposed to prose. The phrase in which Lowell poses her question, "the spectrum of word-values," helps her to confuse the two. Henry B. Fuller begins with verse and ends with poetry. Amid such bewilderments, the plausibility of continuous gradations between the poetic and the prosaic obscured any sharp line that might have been drawn between prose and verse. Since "poetry" implies questions of relative value and obstructs sharp definition, nearly all the theories fell back on comparative distinctions. The perplexity has infected even some writers who look back on the debate from what ought to be a safe distance. Eddie Gay Cone summarizes as follows: "While traditionalists . . . were charging the new poets with writing prose and while experimentalists and their defenders . . . were rebutting with more inclusive distinctions between poetry and prose, Pound and others associated with the Imagists muddied the already murky problem by claiming the influence of prose on poetry to be beneficial" (29, 58). Pound did not "muddy" a problem which he never found murky. Cone succumbs to the habitual form of the old debate. "More inclusive distinctions" were not more decisive or more useful. And Cone misrepresents Pound just as his contemporaries must have done. He did declare, in a dictum taken from Ford Madox Ford, that poetry ought to be at least as well written as prose. But Aiken's paraphrase, "that, in other words, it must be good prose before it can be good poetry," is not a fair one (2, 417). Pound was noting that certain virtues, such as concentration and directness, could be seen as common to both poetry and prose. He was speaking of an aspect of poetry, not verse; not of form, but of style and diction. Indeed, he was one of the few, along with Eliot and Barfield, who consistently distinguished poetry and verse. He warned poets not to "imagine that a thing will 'go' in verse just because it's too dull to go in prose" (87, 6). This makes sense only if prose and verse are opposites, and if poetry has to do with qualities (perhaps opposites of "dullness") one can separate from questions of form.

Pound's model comes close to the one I suggested in my first chapter. It avoids the hopeless disorder I have been ex-

amining here. There is a dichotomy—not a spectrum—
between verse and prose. Lineation distinguishes them.
Robert Bridges touched on this principle before following
Saintsbury into the mire of "expectancy": "Certainly much
well-written free verse, in which the lines are of varying
length and rhythm, is not good prose. However irregular the
lines be, they are conscious of their length: they pose with a
sort of independence and self-sufficiency" (21, 652-53). Vague
as it is, this pierces to a recognizable truth. To use this concep-
tion in analysis, we will need to explore the effects of linea-
tion. For the moment, the simplest and most direct of them
will suit the purpose. I said earlier that verse is harder to read
than prose. One reason is that unless one willfully ignores
lineation, one pauses at the end of each line.[2] Whatever else
this pause may do, it forces the reader to slow down and pay
more attention to what he is reading.

Already certain profits accrue from this way of proceeding.
My definition of "prosody" centers on the control of atten-
tion. If lineation helps to enforce attention, it serves as a pro-
sodic device, whether the line is metrically organized or not.
Furthermore, I related poetry to prosody by calling it "the
language of an act of attention." Drawn together, these terms
answer the question with which I began this chapter: Poetry is
usually written in verse because lineation promotes the atten-
tion which is necessary to prosody and essential to poetry.
(Something else could generate attention. What we call
"poetry" *need* not be in verse. Whether or not it would be rea-
sonable to speak of "prosody" in such cases is beside my
point.) Finally, I asked in the first chapter how free verse,
which abandons metrical conventions, could have a shared
prosody. But lineation itself, which free verse cannot discard
and remain verse, is a convention. The line-end pause it en-
tails is a subsidiary convention, or perhaps a result of the con-
ventions of reading. Even without meter, the poet can count
on sharing these things with his reader. All this looks promis-
ing; it remains to see how well it will perform in concrete
examples.

PROSE AND PROSODY

Before turning to more typical examples in subsequent chapters, I want to risk falling into the "confusion of thought" against which Barfield warned. Once the initial distinctions among poetry, verse and prose have been clearly established, I think we can afford to examine a few interesting "borderline cases."

I take the first from a pair of writers who used scansion to compare verse with prose. Brian Hooker, writing in 1909 before free verse became an issue, discussed "The Rhythmic Relation of Prose and Verse." C. E. Andrews's "The Rhythm of Prose and of Free Verse" appeared nine years later. Both scanned a familiar sentence from Ecclesiastes:

> Remember now thy Creator, in the days of thy
> youth, when the evil days come not, nor the years
> draw nigh, when thou shalt say: I have no pleasure
> in them . . . [Hooker: 49, 425].

(I have substituted my own marks for Hooker's misleading macrons and breves, which he acknowledges are meant "to indicate the presence and absence of stress.")

> Remember now thy Creator, in the days of thy
> youth, when the evil days come not nor the years
> draw nigh when thou shalt say, I have no pleasure in
> them . . . [Andrews: 6, 186].

Though Andrews does not mention his predecessor, the fact that he repeats Hooker's misquotation ("when" for "while" after the first clause) suggests that he knew the earlier article.

Yet their scansions differ. Both use fifteen accents, but in different positions. Andrews seems bent on metrically regular patterns. After the first clause (on which the prosodists agree) he allows only two trisyllabic substitutions in what amount to two lines of iambic pentameter. Clearly he hears the passage

as metrical. It would be easy to connect this phenomenon
with a theory that prevailed among the opponents of free
verse. I have quoted H. E. Warner's formulation: "there is a
sort of rhythm in the most prosaic prose, and as the feeling
which strives to clothe itself in language becomes intense, the
language will become more rhythmic; that is, it will more and
more take on the form of the traditional meters" (102, 91).
But between the theory and Andrews's scansion, it would be
difficult to say which proves which. In either case, proof and
conclusion would circle each other like a dog chasing his tail.
Hooker, on the other hand, shows a fondness for grouped ac-
cents ("days come not," "no pleasure"). And while Andrews,
fascinated by iambic meter, ignores two commas in the origi-
nal text, Hooker adds one and promotes another to a colon.
Dwelling on each word, he seems reluctant to let them slip
away too quickly.

I can spare myself the task of deciding between these scan-
sions by saying that neither one has much to do with prose. In
prose, accent follows sense and syntax. While in traditional
verse the metrical determination of accent helps to control the
interpretation of meaning, in prose the reader can refer only
to his interpretation of meaning, to decide the placement of
accents. Other considerations have some influence. Surely
every clause needs at least one accent, and both ear and tongue
reject any excessive run of unstressed syllables. But the
placement of those accents depends on general conventions of
language. One convention, for instance, determines that in
antitheses (Chicago White Sox / Chicago Cubs) stress falls on
the element that changes, never on that which is repeated.
(The linguistically reasonable answer to the question, "Are
you a fan of the Chicago White Sox?" would be, "No, I prefer
the Boston White Sox.") So, in the passage from Ecclesiastes,
where the conventions of prose suggest no metrical norm,
"days" takes no stress on either occurrence. "Of thy youth"
and "evil," however, both require accents. Furthermore, both
Hooker and Andrews mislead us by abstracting the sentence
from its context. In this part of Ecclesiastes, "remembering"

one's "Creator" is a pervasive theme, and neither word de-
mands stress here in spite of their intrinsic importance.

Thus one might even disagree that there ought to be fifteen
accents. Here is a scansion that uses only seven:

> Remember now thy Creator in the days of thy
> youth, while the evil days come not, nor the years
> draw nigh, when thou shalt say, I have no pleasure
> in them . . .

But if my scansion is no worse than the others, it is no better.
Accent depends on interpretation. Considering what to stress
in "when thou shalt say," I have to choose among the per-
sonal pronoun, the future-tense verb, and the infinitive.
Which is most important: To bring home the point to the
reader personally? To emphasize the disparity between
"now" and "then" on which the whole chapter insists? Or to
imply the subjectivity of both rejoicing and disillusion ("you
say you have no pleasure"), either of which is "vanity"? Ac-
cent is relative, and to stress all three would be to stress none.
But if one could decide firmly among the alternatives, it
would be on grounds far more complex than any general pro-
sodic principle could begin to explain.

To scan prose is in itself a misleading technique. It requires
of the prosodist, and creates in the reader, a kind and degree of
attention that demonstrate the impossibility of distinguishing
clearly between poetry and prose. As we read the sentence
with the attention poetry demands, it becomes poetry; yet it
never ceases to be prose. One could argue that for Hooker and
Andrews scansion has performed the same function as linea-
tion would perform in changing the prose to verse. Both have
read the passage with such concentration that almost every-
thing becomes important in itself, beyond the structure of
significance given it by context. For Andrews, this impor-
tance instinctively takes a metrical form. Surprisingly, it is
Hooker, the earlier writer, who seems to hear the sentence as
a kind of free verse:

Remember now thy Creator,
In the days of thy youth,
When the evil days come not,
Nor the years draw nigh,
When thou shalt say:
I have no pleasure in them . . .

Either technique—scanning prose or turning it into
verse—has the specific effect of increasing the density of ac-
cents. This underlies the general effect of "making it poetry,"
making every possible word individually luminous. The new
accents are easiest to explain in terms of the line-end pause I
mentioned earlier. Three reasons come to mind. First, the en-
ergy required to start again each new line tends to throw un-
wonted stress on one of its first words. Second, surrounded
by silence, each line becomes responsible for maintaining
some internal rhythmic integrity. Since closure or finality
helps to establish that integrity, new stress falls on the ends of
lines. (Neither of these effects is very striking in my lineation
of Hooker's scansion, partly because the lines are so short and
partly because they coincide with syntactical units.) Third,
because the lines break the flow of sense, parallelisms and an-
titheses which prose would subsume into larger rhythmic
units now require stress so as to recall antecedent elements.
(This explains the accents on the two instances of "days.") At
least potentially, accent has a great deal to do with meaning;
and the effects of lineation begin to seem far from trivial.

Perhaps this example loads the question. Biblical chapters
are made up of what we call "verses," suggesting that they
inherently lend themselves to poetic reading. To show that
lineation inevitably influences meaning I need a brief passage
less prepossessing than a sentence from Ecclesiastes. For my
second example I have chosen a clause from Harvey Gross's
Sound and Form in Modern Poetry. Its metaphor makes it inter-
esting to work with, and the homily it presents is appropriate:
"Our 'scansions' lay the lines down in Procrustean beds" (43,
160). By itself it can be read as a rough iambic hexameter,
though an early caesura threatens the metrical stability:

$$\overset{\times}{\text{Our}} \overset{\prime}{\text{'scansions'}} \lVert \overset{\times}{\text{lay}} \overset{\prime}{\text{the}} \overset{\vert}{\text{lines}} \overset{\times}{\text{down}} \overset{\prime}{\text{in}} \overset{\prime}{\text{Procrustean}}$$
beds.

Meter promotes stresses on words which, either because they are somewhat redundant ("lay," whose force is more fully captured in "down") or because the context obviates any special emphasis ("lines"), would probably not be stressed in a prose reading.

I have turned the clause into a line, and the line could be broken at several points.[3] The break that least affects meaning coincides with the hexameter's caesura:

Our 'scansions'
Lay the lines down in Procrustean beds.

Because a caesura implies a syntactical juncture, the new line-end pause adds little to either the hexameter or the prose version. (The same applies to my lineation of Hooker's scansion.) But isolating the second line does emphasize a rhythmic monotony which less obviously damages the hexameter. Its main stresses are strong enough to demote, relatively, any accent on "lines," yielding this result: $/ \text{x x} / \text{x x} / \text{x x} /$. The rollicking, dactylic rhythm seems badly out of joint with the sense, which demands a more constricted, less flighty rhythm. On the other hand, one might take that rhythm as parodic and find a satiric point in the couplet. The Poundian quotation marks around " 'scansions' " ("The pianola 'replaces'/ Sappho's barbitos"), supporting this reading, suggest a great deal about the poem to which these lines might belong.

A slightly stronger break falls in the middle:

Our 'scansions' lay the lines
Down in Procrustean beds.

Here it reverses the demotion of "lines." This helps bring into focus the grammatical object, making the plight of our hapless victims the center of feeling in the metaphor. The new stress on "Down," however, begins to imply an infernal or subterranean Procrustes. This confuses the metaphor and

seems as irrelevant as the passage from Milton it might recall:
"With hideous ruin and cumbustion down/To bottomless
perdition." But a context of surrounding lines could capitalize
on this revision of Procrustes' story by revealing some hidden
relevance—a secret alliance between Hebraic and Hellenic
mythologies that might help to shape the poem. The prosodic
context might well be iambic trimeter. In free verse, the lines'
approximation to a metrical norm could be turned to good
purpose, or could merely distract the reader. Taking these
lines by themselves, of course, we have no way of deciding
whether they are metrical or not.

A third alternative,

> Our 'scansions' lay
> The lines down in Procrustean beds,

creates some confusion. The enjambement implies for a mo-
ment that "lay" is a past-tense intransitive verb, making
"scansions" the Procrustean victim. Another lineation,

> Our 'scansions' lay the lines down
> In Procrustean beds,

removes the ambiguity, but the second line seems too limp.
Its rhythm now diffusely echoes the end of the first line
(though in other versions the comparison escaped notice), and
the whole phrase feels like an afterthought. Once again,
though these two distichs fail in isolation, the right context
could use the implications that either one offers.

After examining the rhythms of these alternative lineations,
especially the first and last, I begin to feel that something is
wrong with the words themselves. One could change them.
The first six contain enough rich, long vowels and inter-
estingly grouped stresses to justify themselves. The problem
seems to lie in "In," a slack syllable that overdoes the conso-
nance on *n*. To paraphrase the last phrase grammatically
would be difficult. "In beds of Procrustes" retains "In" and
feels impossibly awkward. "Like Procrustes," aside from
weakness of diction and rhythmic uncertainty, loses some of

the force of "down" by jettisoning "beds." The Imagist principle of condensation suggests a solution: "Procrustes" could be isolated as an apposition to "scansions." This fulfills the most important function of condensation, which is not to cut down the number of words, but to force the reader's imagination to supply necessary connections (87, 50; 10, 54ff.; 46). Lineation can ease the reader's way:

> Our 'scansions' lay the lines down
> Procrustes . . .

(This recalls the Pound of the *Cantos*.)

> Our 'scansions'
> Lay the lines down
> Procrustes . . .

The final alternative brings out a rhythmic echo, more cogent this time, between "Our 'scansions' " and "Procrustes," and gives " 'scansions' " the emphasis its quotation marks demand. The second line, a trochee followed by a spondee, again suggests Pound, but in his earlier poems.

This experiment has substantiated half of H. E. Warner's declaration that "under the licence of free verse there are a half a dozen ways at least [of dividing a passage into lines], all equally good and none of them changing the value in the least" (102, 92)—and refuted the second half. Each alternative generates different shades of meaning. (William Carlos Williams could completely revise a poem without changing a word [60, 87].) Four of the versions I examined here differ only in lineation. The context, the poem that contained the lines, would decide among them; but it could never find them "all equally good." Arthur Davison Ficke, in one of those attacks on free verse that fade into defenses of rhyme and meter, points out another direction for argument: "Most writers would agree that the exigencies of rhyme suggest felicitous excursions of thought far more frequently than they inhibit the exact statement of an idea in all its original integrity" (36, 11). The assumption that free verse had no means of forcing the poet into "felicitous excursions of thought" helped to justify the charge of "formlessness." Yet it was by manipulating the basic formal resource of all verse, the lineation, that I discovered poetic deficiencies in my original text. The styles that different versions recalled then helped me understand how to remedy the weakness. Not only does Gross's clause in itself suggest a poem; every different arrangement of it suggests an at least slightly different poem. What rhyme and meter can do, lineation alone can also do.

I have been turning prose into verse to show the effects of lineation. With a different purpose, opponents of free verse did the same thing or its opposite. If their favorite charge was "formlessness," their favorite technique was to print free verse as prose. Lacking an adequate sense of the principles violated by that act, Amy Lowell fell into their trap:

> Recently a writer in The Nation [John Livingston Lowes] took some of Meredith's prose and made it into vers libre poems which any poet would have been glad to write. Then he took some of my poems and turned them into prose, with a result which he was kind enough to call beautiful. He then pertinently asked what was the difference. I might answer that there is no difference. Typography is not relevant to the discussion. Whether a thing is written as prose or as verse is immaterial [65].

Lowell's abandonment of the distinction does not increase one's confidence in her poetic ear. Lineation can be well or poorly used, but it can never be "immaterial." Free verse, whatever other resources it may have, is verse; and verse demands that we listen to rhythm if we want to hear what the poem has to say.

Chapter Four

Counterpoint

Listening to the rhythm of a poem entails grasping the princi-
ples that organize it. In my first chapter I concluded that free
verse uses other than numerical principles. As a possible
nonmetrical mode of organization I mentioned the significant
tension among formal patterns, which I called "counter-
point." But such tensions seem to belong to metrical verse.
Traditional verse frequently makes its readers aware of them
by playing off an abstract metrical regularity against the vari-
eties of verbal rhythm, grouping adjacent words with asso-
nance, clinching more distant ones with rhyme, shifting
caesurae from place to place in the line, and so on. These ef-
fects, greatly as they enliven the pleasure a poem gives us, en-
riching our feeling for what it means, rarely strike us as essen-
tial. On the metrical structure that underlies them, poets have
built thousands of different works. A particular poem's inci-
dents of counterpoint seem merely to ornament that unchang-
ing fabric. To understand counterpoint itself as a prosodic
mode, we must reimagine it, see it weaving the fabric anew in
each poem.

A short piece by Louise Bogan provides a good place to
start (18):

THE CUPOLA

A mirror hangs on the wall of the draughty cupola.
Within the depths of glass mix the oak and the beech leaf,
Once held to the boughs' shape, but now to the shape of
    the wind.

Someone has hung the mirror here for no reason,
In the shuttered room, an eye for the drifted leaves,

> For the oak leaf, the beech, a handsbreadth of darkest
>   reflection.
>
> Someone has thought alike of the bough and the wind
> And struck their shape to the wall. Each in its season
> Spills negligent death throughout the abandoned
>   chamber.

Even to call Bogan's poem "meditative" is almost to exag-
gerate the liveliness of its engagement. In the closure of its
segments and the directness and delicacy of its syntax, the
poem refuses to declaim; it scarcely lifts above a whisper dur-
ing its first six lines. Uttering these sentences, a speaker who
is barely more than a voice broods in lofty seclusion above the
living rest of the house. The apparently calm lines balance one
death implied by shapelessness ("the shape of the wind," "the
drifted leaves") with another death imaged by the mirror's
unchanging "darkest reflection" in the "shuttered room."
The voice acknowledges no person but a "someone" whose
act of hanging the mirror had "no reason." Yet in the last
stanza a passion rising behind these rigidly controlled obser-
vations breaks through the restraint to show itself for a
sudden moment. The intensity of the conclusion stands
shockingly against the poem out of which it yet inevitably
develops.

   Part of this development can be traced to the syntactical
structure of the poem. The first line coincides with a sentence.
The remaining two lines of the stanza portion out a second
sentence into separate syntactical units. The second stanza
comprises a third sentence, again divided into three discrete
parts. Each line doles out its contribution to the image in
measured isolation from the others. The line-end pause, al-
ways reinforced by a comma or a period, provides much of
the restraint we feel in the poem; nothing must violate the
boundary of the line. But two sentences split the final three-
line stanza, standing against its pattern without destroying it.
No comma follows "wind," though the enjambement unset-
tles us only slightly. When we reach the period after "wall,"

the motion established by the rest of the poem bids us to stop. Yet the line continues, as though in its sudden fervor the voice could not wait to leap into the next line. When it comes, that leap confronts us with the violence of "Spills negligent death," the speaker's rejection of all the denials the cupola has ranged against her. After the protest has carried one last glance around the "abandoned chamber," a final coincidence of line and sentence closes the poem.

Bogan's method is to dispose various degrees of counterpoint. One might imagine looking through two grids: pieces of window-screen, for instance. When they are perfectly aligned, we see one thick screen. But when one is tilted slightly, a new pattern appears that bears no visual relation to the regular horizontals and verticals of either grid. This pattern—the moiré effect—curves and ripples in the most astonishing ways. The laws that organize each grid, their straight lines and right angles, fail utterly to foretoken the shapes that emerge. As the relation between the grids is again shifted even minutely, different patterns spring into existence. Bogan's words conform to the syntactical grid native to English, though the analogy of a rectangular screen hardly conveys the complexity of that system. Her words also belong to lines. The reader barely notices the separate existence of the first six lines, so directly do they match the syntax. Though they generate attention, they do not shift its focus. But in the last stanza she tilts the sentences in relation to the lines. The effect startles us; and in the context of the whole poem, we interpret the surprise as a sudden passion in the speaking voice.

An obvious question concerns possible "grids" from which the poet can choose. William Carlos Williams's "The Dance," the earlier of two poems by that name, presents an especially odd example (106, 113):

> In Breughel's great picture, The Kermess,
> the dancers go round, they go round and
> around, the squeal and the blare and the

tweedle of bagpipes, a bugle and fiddles
tipping their bellies (round as the thick-
sided glasses whose wash they impound)
their hips and their bellies off balance
to turn them. Kicking and rolling about
the Fair Grounds, swinging their butts, those
shanks must be sound to bear up under such
rollicking measures, prance as they dance
in Breughel's great picture, The Kermess.

Harvey Gross points out that Williams imitates the rhythm of
the dance he describes (43, 121). The triple-time feeling of
anapests or amphibrachs, always infectious, is here so insist-
ent that when only one unstressed syllable intervenes between
stresses, the reading voice automatically compensates with a
rest ("róund ănd /aróund,⁽ˣ⁾ thĕ squéal"). In most cases punc-
tuation helps to locate these rests. Probably a full "measure"
rest follows the first line. In that line, "great" might take an
accent; but by the time the line is repeated as the last, the es-
tablished beat has gained enough power to suppress any em-
phasis on the word. Similarly, the poem sometimes shifts ac-
cents from their normal speech positions ("tŏ bĕar úp ŭndĕr
súch⁽ˣ/ ˣ⁾ róllĭckĭng mĕasŭres"). As I have indicated by using
words like *measure, rest,* and *beat,* the principle is the musical
one of accentual isochrony.

The number of accents in each line varies arbitrarily be-
tween three and four. This rules out an accentual meter. Nor
can I agree with Gross when he speaks of an anapestic meter.
One could mark accented and unaccented syllables, or even
write out a musical scansion; isochrony of accent allows for
that possibility. But any attempt to group the syllables into
feet, whether anapestic or amphibrachic, is frustrated by the
lineation. When feet cross line boundaries, one is clearly deal-
ing with something different from any accentual-syllabic me-
ter. Rather, Williams has constructed a counterpoint between
accentual isochrony and lineation. The isochronous rhythm
might appear to render lineation superfluous or ineffectual.

Yet a prose version of this poem (which would not destroy the isochrony) would be intolerable. A metronomically regular beat does not make for readable prose. The rhythm calls to itself too much attention which it does not reward. The poem needs its lines; but how do they help?

The reader pauses after the first line not only because of syntax and the beat, but because it is so clearly a *line*. Modulating from "g" in "Breughel" and "great" to "k" in "picture" and "Kermess," the sounds of the line hold it together and apart. Throughout the poem, each line makes its own special rhythmic gesture, separable from the metronomic swing of the whole. The fourth line, for instance,

$$\prime \quad \times \quad \times \quad \prime \quad \prime\prime \quad \times \quad \prime \quad \times \quad \times \quad \prime \quad \times$$
tweedle of bagpipes, a bugle and fiddles,

comprises two rhythmic units, identical except that the second has an unstressed syllable for anacrusis, and the first ends with a secondary accent. The units intricately balance one another in sound and sense as well. The sound of "tweedle" at the beginning is answered by "fiddles" at the end. They bracket "bagpipes" and "bugle." Besides these pairs of stressed words, several different groups of three accents (each excluding one of the four) share our attention. The last three name instruments, the first a sound; all but the second end with unstressed consonances on "l"; "bugle" stands alone by posing its open vowel against the pinched "tweedling" of the others. All these overlapping rhythmic patterns, jostling each other like dancers, give the line an internal movement which interests us in its own right. That movement, unique to this line but continuing a series of rhythmically unique lines, counterpoints and enlivens the predominant beat of the poem.

This counterpoint between beat and line corresponds to more general tensions. The "rollicking measures" struggle against the squared-off frame of the poem, which recalls the visual rectangle of Breughel's canvas. (Identical first and last lines reinforce the idea of a frame.) Sight and sound confront each other, just as the still painting quarrels productively with

the raucous motion it represents. Such a confrontation adds
piquancy to many poems about paintings. As "The Dance"
shows, poems appeal ambiguously to both eye and ear. At the
same time, a surprisingly complex syntax unites both linear
and isochronous patterns, even as it cuts across them. To-
gether with the emphasis lines place on oddly chosen words
like "impound," the syntax makes us linger over details. Each
sentence pushes us on toward its end, yet gathers itself into a
structure best understood in spatial terms. Williams tells us as
much about poetry as he does about the painting he takes as
his subject or the dance Breughel takes as his. In all these ways
the prosody of counterpoint helps to weave the meaning of
the poem.

In his later verse, Williams employed what he called the
"variable foot," a term whose mystery I have already noted.
He seems to have meant that each of the three staggered lines
of his stanza should be thought of as one foot, the whole
stanza thus becoming a sort of trimeter line. Though adopting
his terminology would mean embracing confusion, the
theory behind it bears on how one reads Williams's poems.
The "feet" vary in number of syllables and accents; but each
occupies more or less the same amount of time as the rest.
The reader is to adjust his pace according to the length of the
"foot." This is the isochrony of line that Emma Kafalenos ex-
pounds in *Possibilities of Isochrony* (58). Its purpose is clearly to
imitate, with a species of accuracy the poet could not other-
wise attain, the rhythms of speech. Yet for the very reason
that recommends it, the system barely suffices to keep the
poem from losing prosodic control. As I pointed out in the
second chapter, isochronous prosodies run this risk because
all speech tends toward isochrony. Of course Williams im-
itates speech rather than reporting it. Prosodically, he main-
tains this distinction by counterpointing isochrony and syn-
tax. While speech employs both these "grids," it tends to
align them; speaking, we pause at syntactical breaks. But the
poet can make us run over them or pause between them.

The principles of this prosody demand an extended series
of stanzas to develop clearly. This makes it difficult to find a

conveniently brief example in which its effects can be examined. But the first section of Williams's "Shadows" should suffice (106, 157):

Shadows cast by the street light
    under the stars,
        the head is tilted back,
the long shadow of the legs
    presumes a world   5
        taken for granted
on which the cricket trills.
    The hollows of the eyes
        are unpeopled.
Right and left   10
    climb the ladders of night
        as dawn races
to put out the stars.
    That
        is the poetic figure   15
  but we know
    better: what is not now
        will never
be. Sleep secure,
    the little dog in the snapshot   20
        keeps his shrewd eyes
pared. Memory
    is liver than sight.
        A man
looking out,   25
    seeing the shadows—
    it is himself
that can be painlessly amputated
    by a mere shifting
        of the stars.   30
A comfort so easily not to be
    and to be at once one
        with every man.
The night blossoms

        with a thousand shadows   35
              so long
      as there are stars,
          street lights
              or a moon and
      who shall say   40
          by their shadows
      which is different
          from the other
              fat or lean.

If one distinguishes the constant interval of time measuring
each line from the variable pace within it, the relation between
them itself appears as a kind of counterpoint. That relation,
incidentally, resembles the one between meter and rhythm in
accentual-syllabic verse, suggesting that the traditional meter,
too, inherently involves counterpoint. But Williams's poem
derives much of its rhythmic interest from a more complex
counterpoint, changing the relation between its isochronous
lineation—comprising both interval and pace—and its syntax.
In this it resembles highly enjambed blank verse.

The first thirteen lines all coincide with grammatical units,
more or less separable from each other. Even where grammat-
ically related words occupy different lines, each line presents a
recognizable phrase that does not insist on driving us toward
the next. Thus, "taken for granted" (line 6) modifies "world"
in the previous line, but is a self-contained phrase which, in
fact, turns out to be a separable parenthesis. Its insertion keeps
the quick next line ("on which the cricket trills") from attach-
ing itself too ardently to "world," which it modifies more co-
gently than does "taken for granted." Furthermore, "pre-
sumes a world" in itself does not seem to require completion,
and so does not force us on toward these modifying lines.

The slow, emphatic "That/is the poetic figure" announces
the end of this section, whose stately pace is disturbed in the
next ten lines. Strong syntactical breaks (between sentences,
for instance) now break into the middles of lines, and line-end

pauses disrupt syntactical continuities. "[The little dog] keeps his shrewd eyes" (line 21) will not stand alone, and the pause enforced by lineation is no longer calm, but suspenseful. The line demands resolution in "peeled"; we get "pared" instead. A few lines earlier, the break between "will never" (line 18) and "be," lending the latter word unusual stress, distinguishes the verb from the simple copula. "Will never" occupies a line by itself, and requires a long pause at its end to fill out the isochrony. Thus "be" seems to burst out of a silence imposed by furious thought. This whole section suggests a man picking his way through a minefield of words. The remainder of the poem, beginning "A man/looking out,/seeing the shadows" (lines 24-26), returns at least some distance toward the opening pattern, lines and syntactical units slipping back into alignment. Yet because this reflexive moment has intervened, and because symptoms of the disturbance it creates occasionally reappear ("A comfort so easily not to be/and to be at once one/with every man"), the initial calm has disappeared into a sense of urgency.

These shifting relations between syntax and linear isochrony constitute the poem's prosody. Through them, Williams controls the details of our temporal experience in the poem. The counterpoint makes us aware of subtle shifts in tone of voice, implies possible as well as actual developments of the thought that diverge as we watch, slants words in particular ways ("be" means something different each of the three times Williams uses it), and thus contributes with great delicacy to the meaning of the poem. Isochrony alone might do some of this, but not all. If one can distinguish the pace of thought from the more immediately aural pace of speech, isochrony effectively designates only the latter. The fullest function of a prosody is to control both; counterpoint does so.

Williams's use of counterpoint in these two poems depends on unusual systems, employing isochrony of either accent or line. While they clarify the nature of counterpoint, these examples reveal little about common practice in free verse. I want to move toward more familiar ground by citing an un-

likely predecessor for modern poetry. Defenders of free verse
sometimes listed poets they wanted to claim as precursors.
Whitman was the obvious candidate, though his specific pro-
sodic techniques attracted no direct imitation until Allen
Ginsberg turned the long end-stopped lines to his own use.
Blake, Cowley, Arnold, Henley, and MacPherson were men-
tioned for various works (70, 111; 68, 15). Milton's name
came up only because of the metrical experiments he per-
formed in the Choruses of *Samson Agonistes*. In general, Mil-
ton's name was anathema to the New Poets. Every poetic
revolution yearns toward a different past; Pound and, at first,
Eliot refused to embrace the one represented by Milton. Oc-
casionally, a distinct antitraditional bias in modernist think-
ing, partly justifying the fears of critics, could surface in fatu-
ous comments like Richard Aldington's: "Mind, I don't say
that Milton would have been any better if he had employed
free verse; but had he done so, the necessity for concentration
might have struck him, from that the absolute importance of
accuracy, and thence—who knows—he might have discov-
ered poetic style?" (3, 351). Even Pound could speak of Lau-
rence Binyon as "poisoned in the cradle by the abominable
dogbiscuit of Milton's rhetoric" (87, 201).

Yet the example of Milton sheds an unexpected light on
free verse. Perhaps more than any other English poet, he mas-
tered the art of enjambement. In *Paradise Lost* he depended on
"the sense variously drawn out from one Verse into another"
to liberate him from the prosodic convention of rhyme (75,
210). A single sentence will illustrate the point (i, lines 44-49):

> . . . Him the Almighty Power
> Hurl'd headlong flaming from th'Ethereal Sky
> With hideous ruin and combustion down
> To bottomless perdition, there to dwell
> In Adamantine Chains and penal Fire,
> Who durst defy th'Omnipotent to Arms.

Eschewing rhyme, Milton obviously did not abandon all pro-
sodic conventions. Here, he manipulates the accents of his

pentameters less violently than Donne and, with the help of conventional elisions, maintains the decasyllabic norm fairly strictly.

The syntax of this sentence is "unconventional" in the sense that it distorts normal English patterns. Modern poets objected to Milton partly on this ground, since they preferred to reshape syntax through ellipsis rather than inversion (10). But syntax cannot truly reject convention and still exist. Milton invokes the usual forms in the very act of manipulating them in idiosyncratic ways. "Him," at the beginning, recognizably in the objective case, is answered by the subjective "Who" at the end. "th'Omnipotent," whom Satan's attack has forced into the objective, reasserts his control in the subjective case as "the Almighty Power," who governs the whole sentence. The passage enacts both blasphemy and its consequence.

By separating these parallel references with four thick lines, Milton forces us to keep the whole sentence in mind at once in order to comprehend any of it. Thus he imitates the eternal view to which he wants to reawaken his fallen reader. The imitation is paradoxical. Eternity cannot adequately clothe itself in language, which Milton elsewhere calls "process of speech." Here, two sorts of action belie timelessness. The winding stream of the syntax draws us through the sentence from end to end. At the same time, each line creates its own local vortices of energy. To take only one example: "down," ending the third of these lines, belongs grammatically with "Hurl'd" a line before and the prepositional phrase in the line after. But sound connects it with "hideous" and "combustion," sound and etymology with "ruin." In their company it contributes to the line's grand violence.

Thus the passage oddly resembles one of Williams's poems. Though Milton's lines are controlled partly by iambic meter, by distorting the syntax he gives them a self-sustaining force. Their prosody, in a narrow sense of the word, is accentual-syllabic meter; that is their system of rhythmic organization. But within my more general definition, Milton's prosody is counterpoint. It is by manipulating syntax and line and forcing the two into confrontation that he shapes our temporal experience. Distant as he seems from the concerns of the modernists, Milton offers a perspective on nonmetrical prosody. What would happen if one discarded the metrical control of the lines? And what if the poet did not then turn to an isochronous lineation, as in "Shadows," or to the heavy accentual isochrony of "The Dance"? The result would be something like a minimal prosody, controlling rhythm by the counterpoint of lineation and syntax alone.

Surprisingly, several writers have denied that such a counterpoint is even possible. The assumption underlying their position is even more surprising. Graham Hough, for instance, distinguishes free and metered verse in these terms: "What makes a free verse line a line at all? It has no outwardly determined length, as an Alexandrine or an octosyllable has. It is only a line because it is a rhythmical unit, and it is only a rhythmical unit because it is a unit of sense, a unit of syntax" (53, 103). Hough may be misled by thinking of Eliot, whose lines often do coincide with syntactical units: "So, even in such an uncomplicated example as *Prufrock*, almost every line is a sentence, or a grammatical subdivision of a sentence, or a self-contained descriptive phrase, or something of the sort" (53, 104). Robert Bridges similarly approves Edouard Dujardin's declaration that "a line of free verse is a grammatical unit or unity, made of accentual verbal units combining to a rhythmical import, complete in itself and sufficient in itself" (21, 651). What misleads Bridges may be his refusal to discriminate English free verse from French *vers libre*, which derived ultimately from the end-stopped lines of Whitman and influenced those of Eliot. But Sculley Bradley, in "The Fundamental Metrical Principle in Whitman's Poetry," suggests a more interesting source for the error. Whitman realized "that English readers in oral reading had in large measure ceased to observe line-ends or terminal caesurae in verse unless they represented logical pauses. In his desire to be as natural as possible, therefore, Whitman usually constructed his lines as logical units" (20, 443). Bradley implies that, as free verse developed, the line-end pause had first to produce lineation by corresponding to a syntactical pause. Only after its force has been reestablished, perhaps, can the poet assume the pause as a product of lineation and use it to interrupt syntactical units.

The poems of Whitman, and some of Eliot's, show that to equate lines and syntactical units need not entail disaster. But it does limit the rhythmic resources on which free verse can call. Hough shrewdly points this out:

> It is a commonplace that the most powerful effects of traditional verse are achieved by playing off the syntactical movement against the metrical movement—making them coincide very closely as in the Augustan couplet, or making them diverge very widely as in Miltonic blank verse. All this powerful range of effects is closed to free verse, since there is no ideal metrical norm to appeal to. And that is why, I think, we nearly always feel in free verse a certain tenuity and slightness of rhythm, feel it the more the farther we recede from accepted metrical form [53, 104].

Bridges agrees: "The identification of the line unit with the grammatical unit must limit the varieties of line-structure"; monotony results (21, 656). C. E. Andrews, whose prose scansion I examined in the last chapter, concurs (6, 190). More recently, in his article, "Counterpoint," in the *Princeton Encyclopedia of Poetry and Poetics*, Paul Fussell has summarized and adopted the old arguments: "Counterpoint is impossible except in moderately regular metrical compositions, for any variation must have something fixed to vary from" (88, 155). Like the others, Fussell apparently finds it difficult to accept two systems varying mutually, neither one fixed by convention in all details, but systems (and in that sense "fixed") nonetheless.

This is, in fact, one of the oldest, most subtle, and most persistent of objections to free verse. It serves as the basis of

A. D. Hope's attack, which I discussed earlier. And C. E. Andrews allies it with another recurrent argument, about eye and ear and "mere typography": "The poet makes a mistake when he tries to produce in free verse a conflict between the sense phrase and the line. Such a conflict is only evident to the eye. The ear cannot perceive the irregular lines of free verse as separate rhythmical units unless they coincide with the phrase" (6, 192). If Sculley Bradley is right, Andrews's reasoning would have had merit in Whitman's time. But conventions and habits of reading change; and without great difficulty the ear learns to hear what poets have found to say. We read poetry more often than we hear it read. Each experience shapes the other. The silence of our own reading does not prevent the sounds of poetry from affecting us. Our eyes and ears have not been so badly sundered as that. Sound remains as essential to most poetry as any of the other systems that constitute the poem. Seeing the ends of lines, we hear the use to which they are put. As Emma Kafalenos remarks, "if the demand for a pause at the end of every line is accepted, there is no need for the syntactical pause to be positioned at the end of a line. The more complex rhythm produced by placing syntactical pauses in other positions, in a series of adjacent lines, is often desirable" (58, 108). The poets and their readers having reached this agreement, one can see both the desirability and the possibility of counterpoint simply by glancing at a typical page of free verse.

Thus, as Brooks and Warren show, "we find the denial of the prose sentence" by lineation "being set off against recurrent acceptance of the logic of the sentence," as the poem modulates between enjambement and coincidence of phrase and line (23, 175). This prosodic technique informs most free verse, though in different degrees. Louise Bogan's "The Cupola" employs it sparingly. She allows the lineation nearly to disappear into the syntax until her last stanza. The effect resembles those enjambements that Pope reserves for extreme moments; disrupting a uniform texture, any shift startles. But poets frequently reverse the process. W. H. Auden's "Musée des Beaux Arts" exemplifies this more common practice, and more fully demonstrates the adequacy of counterpoint as a prosody. Before examining it in detail, I want to explain how I came upon the illustration it offers.

For an introductory course in modern poetry, I had typed out and mimeographed a set of free-verse poems as if they were prose. My purpose, of course, was not to pretend that the two forms are equivalent, but to broach the fundamental question of how free-verse lines are divided or determined. I asked the students to mark line breaks. The only additional information I gave them about Auden's poem was that it contains two stanzas of unequal length. The nearly unanimous results interested me. Everyone felt that the lines must be relatively long. Furthermore, the lineations they gave were strikingly similar. Here is the poem, as they quite logically arranged it:

> About suffering they were never wrong, the Old
>   Masters:
> how well they understood its human position;
> how it takes place while someone else is eating
> or opening a window or just walking dully along;
> how, when the aged are reverently,
> passionately waiting for the miraculous birth,
> there always must be children
> who did not specially want it to happen,
> skating on a pond at the edge of the wood:
> They never forgot that even the dreadful martyrdom
> must run its course anyhow in a corner,
> some untidy spot
> where the dogs go on with their doggy life
> and the torturer's horse scratches its innocent behind on a
>   tree.
>
> In Breughel's *Icarus*, for instance:
> how everything turns away quite leisurely from the
>   disaster;
> the ploughman may have heard the splash,
> the forsaken cry,
> but for him it was not an important failure;

> the sun shone as it had to on the white legs
> disappearing into the green water;
> and the expensive delicate ship
> that must have seen something amazing,
> a boy falling out of the sky,
> had somewhere to get to and sailed calmly on.

This poem seems to be spoken by someone who has given his lecture many times before—a museum guide, perhaps. His speech has been carefully prepared. It has the elaborate syntax of a set piece. The careful parallelisms may remind us of Whitman. But here the oratory has lost its verve. The speaker himself, wearily reciting the virtues of the tiresome Old Masters, represents the very attitude he describes, turning away "quite leisurely from the disaster." The verse is remarkably dull. This dullness results first of all from redundancy. Lines are divided where syntax, and often punctuation, would divide them anyway. The line breaks enforce accents where syntax would enforce them. Movement from line to line is kept to a slow minimum. The ponderousness of those long clauses cannot make the poem profound in feeling. The diction, casual ("specially," "anyhow," "for instance") and pettily fastidious ("the dreadful martyrdom," "some untidy spot"), contradicts profundity with a trivial tone. This is consistent with what the poem says—that people react this way to others' catastrophes—but it is a bad sort of consistency which exemplifies the "fallacy of imitative form." Form should imitate content, but not by violating everything that makes a poem a poem. An act of attention devoted to inattention walks a thin line, and this poem falls over into insouciance. Whitman made an often brilliant prosody out of oratory, redundancy, and "sameness of structure," but Auden has not done so.

In fact, Auden wrote a much different poem (9):

MUSÉE DES BEAUX ARTS

About suffering they were never wrong,
The Old Masters: how well they understood

Its human position; how it takes place
While someone else is eating or opening a window or
  just walking dully along;
How, when the aged are reverently, passionately waiting
For the miraculous birth, there always must be
Children who did not specially want it to happen,
  skating
On a pond at the edge of the wood:
They never forgot
That even the dreadful martyrdom must run its course
Anyhow in a corner, some untidy spot
Where the dogs go on with their doggy life and the
  torturer's horse
Scratches its innocent behind on a tree.

In Breughel's *Icarus*, for instance: how everything turns
  away
Quite leisurely from the disaster; the ploughman may
Have heard the splash, the forsaken cry,
But for him it was not an important failure; the sun
  shone
As it had to on the white legs disappearing into the green
Water; and the expensive delicate ship that must have
  seen
Something amazing, a boy falling out of the sky,
Had somewhere to get to and sailed calmly on.

In several cases, Auden's lineation generates quite specific
effects which one might call semantic. Some of these depend
on what I described in the last chapter as a principle of an-
tithesis, that changing elements take stress and constant ones
do not. The reverse applies as well: Where a word is unex-
pectedly stressed, it suggests the alternatives from among
which it has been chosen. In this poem, the unexpected
stresses are created by line breaks. The division of "how well
they understood/Its human position" gives "human" a force
it would not claim in prose. That force makes us aware of
what the poet excludes. Suffering, for instance, does not have

an animal position. (The animals he mentions later in the
stanza help to suggest this alternative.) Animals suffer; but
not, we assume, in the same way as humans. Their pain lacks
the imaginative complexity of human pain. And to suffer
martyrdom, death for a religious idea, is something no animal
would either choose for itself or think to inflict on another.
By the same token, suffering does not belong to the divine.
The savior whose "miraculous birth" prefigures his eventual
"dreadful martyrdom" must be essentially human. These ex-
clusions help to define precisely what Auden wants "suffer-
ing" to mean in the poem. The information derives from an
accent created by lineation.

Similarly, a new stress on "Children" directs our attention
to its antithesis with "the aged," whose reverent, passionate
waiting stands against their nonchalance. "The miraculous
birth" enters into the same complex of meaning. So close to
their own (unmiraculous?) births, these children ignore one
that has special significance for them. The new child will
grow, not only into their savior, but into a savior especially
interested in children. "Suffer the little children to come unto
me" springs to mind. More important, the warning that to
enter the kingdom of Heaven we must become "as little chil-
dren" embodies the revolutionary idea of children as models
of innocence. In Auden's poem, innocence manifests itself as
naive indifference, blameless but finally disastrous.

Turning from the line breaks to the lines they create, we
feel a different sort of effect. The fourth line imitates, by its
length and paratactic structure, the tedium which the whole
poem discusses and which too thoroughly infects the other
version I presented. It is this poem's longest line. The shortest
is "They never forgot," whose slightness and redundancy
might seem not to justify it as a line. But we must pause in
reading it to remember that "They" are "the Old Masters,"
not the children or the aged, and to understand that we are
being returned to our starting point. The pause makes us
aware that the whole first stanza pivots, on this line, between
two divisions of its general topic. Another line groups the

animals, the dogs and the torturer's horse. Yet another iso-
lates "a pond at the edge of the wood" as a detail sufficiently
pictorial (and reminiscent of Breughel) to prepare us for the
painting that the second stanza will describe.

The second stanza begins to increase the intensity of the
verse in preparation for ending. Effects similar to those of the
first stanza reappear, as the line breaks more and more radi-
cally contradict syntactical pauses. Sometimes they promote
stress on quite ordinary words:

> . . . the ploughman máy [or may not]
> Have heárd the splash,

but could hardly *see* anything so minute and out of the way,
nor be bothered to turn to look at it.

> For hím it was not an important failure,

though it was for Icarus, and though it turned man's first at-
tempt at flight into disaster. The sun, which had melted the
binding wax in Icarus' wings, "shone/As it hád to," denying
both malice and mercy in perfect indifference. These divi-
sions, and others like them ("the green/Water," "must have
seen/Something amazing"), strike us first of all as peculiar.
This oddness itself creates the kind of attention to detail that
lineation contributes to prosody. It helps us notice the nearly
subliminal rhyme, which further reinforces the lines' endings
as they stand against the syntax. Rhyme organizes the first
stanza only loosely: *a b x a c d c b e f e f d*. Supporting the gen-
eral tightening of the poem toward its conclusion, the rhymes
of the second stanza hold to a sticter pattern: *a a b c d d b c*.

Finally, the line breaks force the poem's speech away from
the boredom that weighs it down in prose or in my false linea-
tion, and toward a kind of celebration. The weary museum
guide still speaks; the diction and the syntax belong to him.
But a moment's awe begins to inspire him despite all his ex-
perience. An analogy may help. Breughel's painting, "The
Fall of Icarus," shows us a landscape with water in the middle
distance, a ship on the water and, dominating the whole

scene, a burly peasant and his ox, who seem to belong to the
ground they plow. In one corner, an incidental detail, two
pale legs protrude from the waves. Yet in naming his painting
Breughel thought not of the plowman or the landscape but of
the legs. If the speech of Auden's museum guide resembles
the painting itself and adopts its perspective on the scene, then
the gesture of Auden's lineation matches that of Breughel's
title.

The tone that finally emerges from Auden's poem exceeds
in complexity anything his words themselves seem to offer.
The moiré effect of counterpoint creates patterns of meaning
which its components alone cannot explain. The speaker is
pompous and compassionate, amused and awed. His own
irony wearies him; yet something in the painting he has seen
so many times suddenly sharpens his eye for "the expensive,
delicate ship" and "the green/Water," for all that is "amaz-
ing." His fatalism ("must run its course," "as it had to") is
somehow tinged with joy. The effect increases in the second
stanza, where line and phrase conflict most sharply. The tone
implied by lineation does not destroy the one embodied in
syntax and diction, but complicates it. At the same time,
Auden allows line and snytax to coincide whenever he wants
to close off a section of the poem. The points where periods,
semicolons, or colons end lines indicate the divisions in the
subject. The end of the poem employs a more complex tech-
nique of closure as well:

> Something amazing, a boy falling out of the sky,
> Had somewhere to get to and sailed calmly on.

Each of these last two lines begins by tying up a syntactical
loose end. By shifting the relation of line and syntax between
such coincidences and pointed confrontations, the poet con-
trols our movement through the poem. All these effects,
semantic and tonal and rhythmic, belong essentially to pros-
ody. "Musée des Beaux Arts" depends only on counterpoint
for its prosody; but that is enough.

Chapter Five

The Discovery of Form

The arts which control the material and possess the
necessary knowledge are two: the art which uses the
product and the art of the master-craftsman who directs
the manufacture. Hence the art of the user also may in a
sense be called the master-art; the difference is that this
art is concerned with knowing the form, the other,
which is supreme as controlling the manufacture, with
knowing the material.

Aristotle, *Physics*

In all that precedes, I have tried to show that to perform its
basic function prosody does not require meter. Nonmetrical
prosodies can create and focus attention, and thus contribute
intricately to the meaning of a poem. Yet poets could discover
this possibility only by recognizing that any prosody has to
depend on conventions shared with readers. Using free verse
did not simply mean discarding metrical principles but sub-
stituting new ones. Often the conventions on which these
new principles rest, such as lineation itself and its relation to
syntactical rhythms, are at once less obvious (less explicitly
systematic) and more fundamental than the special conven-
tions of meters. In this sense, the invention of free verse re-
quired, and implies, a new awareness of prosody as part of the
communication a poem offers to its readers. Besides allowing
poets to use new techniques prosodically, this awareness has
also encouraged directly rhetorical uses of form to establish a
special community between the maker of the poem and the
reader who "uses" it.

A short poem by Wallace Stevens will let us explore this
rhetorical effect (96):

VALLEY CANDLE

My candle burned alone in an immense valley.
Beams of the huge night converged upon it,
Until the wind blew.
Then beams of the huge night
Converged upon its image
Until the wind blew.

Such a poem does not confuse us through obscure language, but through the opacity of its significance. What it says is clear; what it means is mysterious. We are puzzled, that is, about *why* the poem says what it says. As with some technical text in a discipline we know too dimly, our first impulse may be to seek out the sense of each word and string these together. Thus the critic could begin by treating the poem as what Hi Simons calls a "radical" metaphor, one that leaves its tenor wholly to implication (94, 52). If he can identify the missing tenor, he will find himself on the familiar ground of "figurative language," holding the key to the cipher. Several critics have adopted this method. They speak of the candle as "the illuminating power of the creative artist" or as "the power of the imagination" (64, 83; 16, 83). "The candle," says one, "like the romantic ego, stands amid process, and while it brings the world to order around it, this is anything but permanent" (90, 63). But the vagueness and multiplicity of these interpretations (rather than any definite inaccuracy; they answer rightly the wrong question) suggest that we will not locate the poem's meaning by identifying nouns piecemeal ("candle" equals "imagination," "night" equals "process"). This approach fails, as with the specialized text; we lack the context of knowledge that would resolve the conglomeration of terms and show us how they modify each other.

Instead, we must search out the circumstances of the utterance. That is the context in which the poem will make sense. This search involves questions about the speaker—why he speaks, the situation in which he speaks, and so on—none of which the poem answers directly. Its speaker describes events, but not himself. Examined for clues, what he says leads nowhere. Yet he has left us another clue in the *way* he says it. Faced with a mysterious collection of words, individually indeterminate, we step back to see the shape of the whole. Baffled by an obscure content, we seek the meaning of the utterance in its structure.

When we face it squarely, we see that the structure is characterized chiefly by massive repetition. Of the poem's entire second half, only "Then" and "its image" are not repeated from the first half. The whole work consists of an introductory line presenting an object and its setting, two lines describing an event, and three lines dividing and repeating those two with a new grammatical object. (The break between lines 4 and 5, aside from manageability of length, serves the purposes of rhythmic integrity and closure.) It is only the first line that asks us to think at all about what this "valley candle" stands for. "Alone"; "an immense valley"; the sharp austerity of the image and its almost surreal juxtaposition of a tiny artificial thing with a vast natural one; and above all "*My* candle": all invite interpretation as emblems. But they do not demand it, nor do they allow us to satisfy this first simple kind of curiosity. The line can be taken—and by default must be—simply as setting the poem's action. Its oddities work mainly as ways of honing our concentration. The remaining lines do not even invite emblematic interpretation, but play out their gesture of repetition almost abstractly.

This gesture calls attention to the single significant variation between the two halves. The wind blows out first the candle, then the candle's "image." (The absence of an expected comma after "image," quickening the enjambement, encourages extra stress.) The candle, like the wind, is external or objective. The candle's image—on the retina? in the memory?—resides in some faculty of the perceiving mind; it is subjective. (The structure of the statement, and that alone, brings this dualism into the poem. The image itself has nothing to say about modes of thought.) Yet, although the action of the second half is internal to the speaker, the external force of the wind is said to retain its power. This suggests a confusion or interdependence—the poem's conciseness and its finicky diction, belonging more to a philosopher than a madman, indicate the latter—of imagination and external reality. This interdependence obviates the difficult questions one might be tempted to ask about whether the events are literal or symbolic. It also yields an explanation for the odd phrase, "Beams of the huge night." The phrase in itself implies some kind of exchange or reciprocity, since it assigns to darkness a word normally applied to light. Just as the imagined or remembered candle responds to the objective force of the wind, so the candle's artificial light apparently commands a response from the night, even when the light is imaginary. "Imaginary" and "real" become not antonyms but synonyms. The night responds by accepting order, since "beams" are more coherent than the apparently "real" amorphousness of night. This is also one connotation of "converge"—though on repetition lineation emphasizes the word to complicate this with a more hostile tone.

The word "form" sometimes suggests *merely* "the way the thing is said"—simply ornamenting some distinct "content" which, by contrast, carries meaning on its own honest face. But this dichotomy fails when meaning adheres instead to some interface between "form" and "content." Reading "Valley Candle," we do not deduce a theme and then appreciate how deftly Stevens uses form. We examine the form and from it abstract a theme: that when internal and external experience have identical structures, subjects and objects become interchangeable. Whether one equates the "valley candle" with "the creative artist" or "the power of the imagination," or merely identifies it as a human artifact, turns out to be nearly irrelevant. (If anything, one would prefer what Frye calls "identification *as*" to "identification *with*" the artist or the imagination [40, 170]. The candle, remaining itself, embeds itself in the poem, and we avoid abstracting it for separate interpretation.) What matters instead is a particular gesture of thought, which might take any materials for its embodiment—a jar in Tennessee, for instance, or the eye of a blackbird among mountains. The image or (perhaps) metaphor of the candle may be the poem's content or material; but the poem's meaning depends on an "act of the mind" as it perceives its own relation to the world. The poem represents two events in identical language because they are identical in structure. Thus the linguistic repetition precisely reflects the theme. The form actively guides our attention to what signifies (the gesture of thought) and away from what does not (the object chosen to manifest it). Yet the form of repetition-with-variation cannot exist without *some* object. In short, form and content are inseparable. This is a commonplace; the poem exhibits "unity," meshing its formal and material causes.

Yet the formal cause is equally linked with an efficient cause, the maker—or rather the making—of the poem.[1] Meaning arises not from what the poem says, but from what it does and the doing that it represents. It cannot be reduced to either a content (a set of propositions) or a form, in the sense in which that word complements "content"—an achieved product, a static structure. Nor, indeed, can meaning be reduced to an accomplished combination or unity of form and content. We comprehend the poem only as a process, not as an object. (Howard Nemerov has remarked that a poem is less a thought than a mind, thinking.[2]) "My candle," confronting "the huge night," is no single abstracted faculty of the human mind, but the speaker himself in his act of speaking. Though this, too, appears to be a sort of "identification *with*," this equation does not express meaning directly, as phrases like "the power of the imagination" try to do. It gives us not the concluded meaning of the poem but a way of reading it—"meaning" as a participle, not a noun. This process of reading is controlled by the poet: He gives us a model to follow, a process to imitate. This model is form. The form of "Valley Candle" encourages us to identify with the implied author's experience by reducing our separation from him, since the form is as new to him as it is to us. (The poem reports—inaccessibly—the author's experience; but it *is* the experience of the implied author.) The form convinces us that the experience we share is unique: If this has happened before, and if the form is an integral part of its happening, why have we never seen the form before? Yet if the form were entirely unique, the poem would be entirely incomprehensible. At the same time, then, it allows us to infer the universality of the experience. As in many of Stevens's poems, the whole piece might be prefaced by "For instance." The simultaneous novelty and accessibility of the form, subordinating the particular choice of content, imply that we are undergoing not just an experience but a *kind* of experience. The discovery we witness and share is of something always ready to happen.

"Discovery" seems the best name for this whole experience or process or rhetorical method. "Discovered form" is not a form, but a way of thinking about poetic forms. It presents form not as product but as process, not as structure but as operation. Another name would be "organic." But this venerable term has two disadvantages. First, it has been used so often and so loosely as to mean little more than "good." More subtly, it has two implications that have diverged misleadingly. Coleridge (quoting Schlegel) introduced the term to define comprehensively all poetic form.[3] It implied both the unity of form (in the sense of structure) with content, and a theory of the genesis of poems. Keats expressed this theory by demanding that poetry come to the poet "as naturally as leaves to a tree" (59). But modern critics, particularly since Wimsatt and Beardsley published their attack on the "Intentional Fallacy," have avoided speculating about the origins of poems, and so tended to ignore this second implication.[4] "Organicism" originally attributed to the poem a life of its own; but when reduced to a simple matter of unity, the principle encourages one to treat the poem as an object, something to be observed more than participated in. It seems important to restore the original force of the idea.

I do not mean to dispute the arguments against the Intentional Fallacy. And yet, as Wayne Booth has recognized by inventing the term "implied author," the reader cannot help but believe that the poem comes from somewhere. He will invent a speaker if none is named; and the poet leaves him clues on which to build. In "Valley Candle," Stevens erases the distinction between unity (the seamless product given to our inspection) and genesis, by making his poem accessible only as a process, at once "his" and the reader's. "Organic form" having lost its full meaning, a form that presents itself this way can be called "discovered." The word implies both invention and revelation. The fact that "invention" can in turn mean either finding or creating will concern us later. At the moment, the point is that such a form represents an experience shared by the reader and the poet—or at least the poet's mimetic representative in the poem, the speaker.

The shared assumptions that underlie any prosody naturally attach themselves to this experience, and help to constitute it. The unique structure of "Valley Candle" lends poignancy and immediacy to our impression of discovery. For a poet seeking this effect, free verse seems a logical strategy. But it is not the only one. Though discovered (*né* "organic") form is not *a form* but a way of reading, the theory has influenced poets' choice of particular forms at least since Coleridge named it. We might pause to explore a little of this prosodic history.

From the beginning, the "organic" theory carried within it the seeds of prosodic change. The Romantic poet could demonstrate his sincerity by seeking more open structures than those his predecessors had used.[5] Comparison of Wordsworth's blank verse with Milton's reveals a progressive tendency to loosen established metrical kinds. The Romantics also tended, in many instances, to prefer inherently loose forms like the verse-epistle to elaborate structures like Sidney's double sestinas or the telegraphic epigrams of Pope's couplets. T. S. Eliot was probably wrong to say that "the decay of intricate formal patterns has nothing to do with the advent of *vers libre*," though certainly it "had set in long before" (35, 36).

Free verse did not cause the "decay," but represented a later
stage of the same movement. ("Decay" begs the question,
and Eliot's whole statement needs qualification. Though the
abandonment of meter has served bad poets as an excuse for
formlessness—just as meter may conceal vacuity—some of
the prosodic structures used in free verse, as I have tried to
show, are as intricate in their own ways as forms that rely on
elaborate abstract principles.) In the meantime, adjusting the
relation between form and content came more and more to
mean adjusting form *to* content.

Coleridge's own "Christabel," employing a "new" accen-
tual meter, accommodates his archaic, balladlike subject. As
one might expect from so early a trial, the accommodation
does not entirely succeed; but the poem represents an experi-
mental impulse, which in turn indicates dissatisfaction with
given, traditional forms. Yet except for Blake (who first ex-
tended iambics almost to the breaking length and later ex-
changed them for syntactically ordered lines like Whitman's),
Coleridge alone among the first Romantics even temporarily
abandoned accentual-syllabic meter. Those who loosened
form to achieve an "organic" effect at first confined their at-
tention to the higher levels of organization. Blank verse
tended to replace the heroic couplet. Keats preferred to invent
the stanza of "Ode to a Nightingale" rather than adopt some
traditional stanzaic structure. The ode itself traditionally of-
fered a freedom that the Romantics welcomed. More subtly,
Keats preferred for "The Eve of St. Agnes" (and Byron for
"Childe Harold") the distinctive medievalism of Spenser's
stanza, rather than some newer, freer, yet more currently
familiar pattern. So far, the "organicist" criterion did not turn
poets away from prosodies with received and abstract princi-
ples, but only outmoded some larger structures traditionally
built out of those prosodies.

Hopkins and Browning, who loosened the iambic line to-
ward its accentual and syllabic poles, respectively, inherited
this tendency to adjust metrical form for the sake of content
or the authenticity of the individual voice. They came closer

than most of their predecessors to breaking the hegemony of accentual-syllabic principles. It was Whitman, however, who most fully realized the possibilities of "organicism," not merely by treating prosody in new ways, but by creating a new kind of prosody. "His one most consistent rationalization of his technique," according to Gay Wilson Allen, "was that the thought and the form must always exactly coincide" (5, 217-18). This was Coleridge's idea and, in America, Emerson's. Whitman's contribution was to insist on applying it radically to prosody. He replaced given forms, including meter, with discovered or invented ones, to communicate his democratic vision and underscore his tone of continual exploration. Each poem, sometimes each line, had its own prosody, though since his general prosodic principles remained as consistent as his "rationalization," it might be more accurate to say that he intended each *poet* to have an individual prosody. Insisting on "organicism" and demonstrating that an entirely nonmetrical prosody could enhance that effect, Whitman helped to inspire the modern free-verse movement.

The issues in the controversy occasioned by that movement all revolved around the nature of poetic form. This is why one must trace them back a century before they emerged explicitly. The force of Coleridge's definition of "organic form," both in his original expression of it and in its ultimate effect, was to generate a new awareness of form. Eddie Gay Cone, summarizing the controversy, stresses this fundamental question: "Defenders of free verse saw that usually its critics . . . thought not really in terms of form at all but of forms, a list of inherited patterns into which any true poem must correctly fit" (29, 137). Such doctrines as Pound's "tenets of Imagism" imply an "organicist" poetics, which opposes absolutely the notion that, as H. E. Warner said in attacking free verse, "in almost all cases the thought can be more adequately given in prose than in poetry" (103). No matter what his specific formal decisions, the poet after Coleridge understands form less as a box than an incarnation. Complementing the "idea"—less content than matter—the form constitutes its *only* adequate expression.[6] Shakespeare would surely have agreed, if he had thought in such terms; but only after about 1800 did the question become likely to arise. Once it did, it finally instigated formal experiments more radical than contemporaries of Coleridge needed or desired.

Before I turn to further examples of these experiments, one general point about modern prosodic history needs to be made. The criterion of discovery could be taken to militate against any use of received forms. During and after the great controversy, many poets understood it in that way. Some, like Williams, developed the possibilities of free verse almost exclusively. But even for Whitman, as for Coleridge reviving accentualism and Byron the Spenserian stanza, finding new forms usually meant returning to very old ones which had fallen out of use. As it influences the choice of forms, discovery implies freshness, not absolute newness; depending as they do on conventions, prosodies cannot embrace complete novelty. Whitman (and perhaps Blake) turned all the way back to the versicles of the Bible. Later, the less distant traditional forms—metrical forms—could also be rediscovered.

How this rediscovery works will occupy my next chapter, but its public history can be summarized quickly. Robert Bridges saw all forms as balancing convention with discovery. That the writer of free verse can count on obtaining certain effects by the use of certain rhythmic devices, he argued, "implies that they are what other ears are prepared to accept, and such effects can only be the primary movements of rhythm upon which all verse has always depended" (21, 653). "What other ears are prepared to accept" is conventional. But "the primary movements of rhythm" must have been discovered somewhere in the poetic material or in the human ear or soul or nervous system. Pound claimed that the sonnet exemplified such a discovery. It "occurred automatically when some chap got stuck in the effort to make a canzone. His 'genius' consisted in the recognition of the fact that he had come to the end of his subject matter" (87, 168). Even near the revolutionary beginning (1918), Pound acknowledged that a traditional meter could sometimes be the "absolute rhythm" he sought in each poem.[7] He believed "that most symmetrical [i.e., metrical] forms have certain uses [although] a vast number of subjects cannot be precisely, and therefore not properly rendered in symmetrical forms" (87, 9). It was a question of choosing among available alternatives, not of bowing to the dictates of any convention that could not accommodate the particular character of the individual poem.

Free verse simply presented the most radical alternative, and many poets chose not to avail themselves of it. When they began to see free verse as a fad, Pound and Eliot, its first great champions, experimented for a time with iambic tetrameter quatrains. (Eliot's "The Hippopotamus" is an obvious example; Pound's "Hugh Selwyn Mauberley" provides more tangential ones [43, 147-51].) Yet even the metrical work of modern poets demands that we notice the prosodic choices being made. Yeats's "No Second Troy" is not a sonnet, not because it lacks two lines, but because his subject did not accord with the movement implied by the sonnet form. Without stopping to complain (as Keats did in "On the Sonnet") that one received form too much constrained him, he chose the more "precisely" and "properly" (as Pound says) suitable alternative of enjambed quatrains. In "Leda and the Swan," the accord did exist—though the poem also extended the possibilities of the sonnet. The thrust and return of its thought, its movement from concrete action to meditation on the action, called for the sonnet form, as the steady accumulation of impassioned questions in "No Second Troy" did not. (Of course, we cannot actually know whether the choice of form preceded or followed the evolution of the thought.) Similarly, the new awareness of form that produced free verse led also to the apparently opposite result: Any anthology of modern poetry exhibits a whole catalogue of villanelles, sestinas, ballades, and so on. Finally, I would argue that the writing of metrical verse was generally improved by the whole atmosphere of new and experimental attention to form. Richard

Aldington assumed so in his fatuous remark that if Milton
had written free verse he might have written better; but by
comparing the metrical verse published between 1930 and
1940 with that published between 1900 and 1910 one could
find less dubious evidence that the ways of thinking about
form encouraged by the possibility of free verse benefited
metrical verse as well.

Still, the principle of discovered form has a special bearing
on nonmetrical prosody. Its most far-reaching effect is to
create the possibility—or, when carried to a dogmatic ex-
treme, the necessity—of a prosody that will shift in its details
from one line to the next, as the poem demands. Organic
form, said Coleridge, "shapes, as it develops, itself from
within," arising "out of the properties of the material." Amy
Lowell, after analyzing one of her own poems, claimed that
she used free verse because "these delicate variations of
movement, or rhythm, if one prefer that term, have always
been possible to music, but poetry had no power of express-
ing them until the introduction of cadenced verse" (73, 139).
Though Lowell grossly overstates the case, "organicism" or
discovery can be seen as requiring a new prosodic flexibility.
Each line can and must make its own rhythmic statement; it
must have some particular weight. When rhythm renounces
the support of abstract or independent systems—meter or
isochrony—the basic principle of the line emerges and takes
absolute control: Not time alone, nor accent alone, but a
combination from among all the elements of sound and of
sense must give the line some special twist to justify its indi-
vidual existence. The details of its rhythm are discovered (by
poet and reader) with what it says; they are "organically"
united.

Beyond this, the poem as a whole must establish some gen-
eral prosodic scheme, a framework within which the gestures
of individual lines take on meaning. This is how the prosodies
of counterpoint work, which I examined in the fourth chap-
ter. Lineation and syntax provide the poem's general prosody
by counterpointing each other; but specific lineations are de-

termined by the exigencies of context and, finally, by the poet's ear. Just as the poet finds his place between convention and discovery—tradition and the individual talent—so his lines balance contextual constraint and autonomy. Their authenticity derives from his, and their rhythm becomes "absolute." Freed from meter, but faithfully tracing the shape of poetic perception, the line also fulfills the second, genetic half of the "organic" theory.

Two short poems by Williams will show how lines are determined by context and material. The first of them exemplifies the kind of discovered form that derives from and maintains the appearance of spontaneity. But the imitation of spontaneity threatens the poem with looseness, inconsequence, and incoherence; and "Exercise" (105, 15) also shows how sufficient care and skill in lineation can obviate these threats.

EXERCISE

Maybe it's his wife
the car is an official car
belonging

to a petty police officer
I think
but her get-up

was far from official
for that time
of day

If the propositions of Stevens's "Valley Candle" mystify us as hermetic oracles, those of "Exercise" resemble the mere inanities of gossip. In both cases, while the saying is clear, the significance is elusive. If Williams had written it in prose, we would feel no reward in reading it. Yet by presenting it as a poem, he claims it to be, in Auden's phrase, memorable speech. Only by lineation can it justify that claim.

The simplest function of line divisions is to substitute for punctuation. Williams uses his first line-break this way. "Maybe it's his wife" stands grammatically apart from the sentence that constitutes the rest of the poem. We supply a missing period, or at least a colon or semicolon. This is our first signal, not only that lineation will give this utterance a structure more organized than that of prose (will serve as a prosody), but that syntax—the system more obviously allied with "content"—will be subordinated to lineation. Williams uses the lack of punctuation to focus our attention on the form—specifically, on the structures that the lines create for themselves. These tend to be organizations by symmetrical arrangement rather than the numerical organizations by correspondence to an abstract pattern which define meter. Thus the first line is rhythmically symmetrical:

Maybe it's his wife.

Why could this line not have been divided another way? A break must follow "wife," but could the line not have been two? Here one begins to see how lineation can establish the structure of a poem's *sense*, or, to put it differently, how it can serve as a form that both organizes and arises from the words. The only probable place to break the line is after the first word. (Any other division produces mere melodrama.) But to open the poem "Maybe/it's his wife" would alter its meaning. The poem expresses doubt, but not exactly about the woman's identity. To split this line would be to throw doubt on the premise, the simple identification of the woman as the policeman's wife, by making us too intensely conscious of doubt too soon. Instead, Williams chooses a lineation that allows uncertainty to be diffused gradually over the whole poem. This shifts the doubt to the woman's behavior, which is dubious partly because she *is* "his wife."

The second line is also symmetrical, or nearly. (Another moment's thought about alternatives explains why "the" introduces the line. It has no reason to stand alone; and to attach it to the previous line, besides disturbing the function of the first line break, would create a rhythmic impetus too unstable for so early a point in the poem. Furthermore, this very approximateness of symmetry enhances the reader's sense of discovered form as spontaneous improvisation. This is also one function of Williams's title.) Though the repetition of "car" imitates the accentuation of line 1, the stress pattern is reversed, the strongest stress now moved to the middle of the line:

the cár is an officíal cár

The third line, to which I will return, duplicates this pattern while reducing it:

belónging

Line 4 picks up the strongly stressed "official" from line 2 as "officer," and introduces yet another principle of order by alliterating on "p" and "c," a principle used again in line 7 ("was far from official"). The stress in line 4 is more or less medial.

The fifth line, "I think," is isolated partly for reasons of punctuation, like the first. But it stands apart as the only line in which the poet makes his own presence explicit. Placing this single self-reference squarely in the midst of the middle stanza, he imitates on a larger scale the pattern of previous lines, stress falling medially in a rhythmic unit. Syntactically, it could have gone elsewhere. Actually, the preceding lines obey two apparently opposite patterns—the first strung between its ends, the second through fourth gathered about their strong middles—though both are symmetrical. Paradoxically, both apply to the poet's position in his poem, so that his placement of line 5 summarizes the rhythmic character of the whole first half. As the perceiving intellect, he stands at the center; but conscious attention is directed toward the surrounding objects of his perception. Yet one's chief interest in the poem—especially a poem that calls itself "Exercise"—is the ordering act of perception itself. This is the act—the discovery—we share mimetically with the poet as speaker.[8] His apparent abnegation of self-importance is not meant to conceal his indispensability.

"Get-up" is the dynamic word in line 6. The most loaded word in the poem, and its most striking Americanism, it expresses disapproval, or at least implies that the woman's garb (we are not told what it is; the opposite hypotheses of night-gown and evening gown seem equally probable) is the reverse of "official." "Official" has already been repeated once as "officer," and it returns in line 7. Both the sixth and seventh lines display a new structure, not symmetrical, in which the important stress comes at or near the end, the rest of the line serving as rhythmic and semantic introduction. (Line 4 begins to hint at this displacement of accent; and if line 5 receives any stress at all, it is terminal.) In pace, this pattern better suits the end of the poem than would the balance of the first lines. It pushes on toward a climax, reached at the last "official." As the fifth line rhythmically summarized the poem's first half (and as the third echoed the second), so this rhythm reflects in miniature the movement of the whole poem. On the other hand, by dividing the last phrase into two lines, Williams achieves the opposite but equally necessary rhythmic effect of slowing down the poem's thrust so as to make closure more convincing. A secondary reason for this division becomes evident if one tries to combine the lines:

$$\overset{\times}{\text{was}} \; \overset{\prime}{\text{far}} \; \overset{\times}{\text{from}} \; \overset{\times}{\text{of}}\overset{\prime}{\text{fi}}\overset{\times}{\text{cial}}$$

$$\overset{\times}{\text{for}} \; \overset{\prime}{\text{that}} \; \overset{\times}{\text{time}} \; \overset{\times}{\text{of}} \; \overset{\prime}{\text{day}}$$

would make—in this context—an annoying jingle. While in metrical verse such rhythmic regularity conveys certainty almost independently, this kind of free verse claims to discover rhythmic form directly, moment by moment, within the developing sense of the words and meaning of the poem to which the rhythm itself is contributing. The regularity would feel extraneous.

"Exercise" justifies this claim to a discovery of form by convincing us that we share with the poet an immediate experience. We recognize the progression that the lines enact—from balance to motion to closure—as a pattern of action and thought. It is the progression, for instance, followed by the experience of perceiving something, wondering about it, and (with or without a definite conclusion) turning away from it. (Note the shift to past tense at line 7, when the car has passed. By this simple device Williams gives the poem a plot, projecting its rhythmic shape into narrative. Thus he welds the time of the event, which only he experiences, to the time of the poem, which we share with him.) Simultaneously, the gesture of improvisation made by "discovered" free verse tends to justify informality in punctuation, which allows Williams to leave the last line open and thus to imply the continuity of this experience with others—with further conversation, for instance. These two kinds of imitation, taken together, will stand for Williams's conception of poetry in general: It isolates an individual experience so as to order it and give it significance; at the same time it remains true to the incessant world that does not sanction the isolation of one action or perception from another. Like his free verse, Williams's poetry represents for him an order discovered within or wrenched from disorder.

Thus the opposition of "get-up" and "official," an ordered pair plucked from a welter of perceptions and memories. This is one of the key structures in the poem, and the positions of these words in their respective lines, stressing them and thus their opposition, show the primary importance of lineation in defining the poem's meaning. And only lineation convinces the reader to pay special attention to a word that has no great syntactical power within the sentence: "belonging." (To repeat: The function of prosody is to control attention.) Given that attention, the word reveals itself as the only strong verb in the poem; except for "I think"—separated for reasons I have already discussed—all the other verbs are copulae. The verb, "to belong," as a statement of relationship, becomes a node from which much of the poem's meaning radiates. In its immediate grammatical context, it tells us that the car belongs to the officer, as the attributive adjective "official" also suggests. The woman, in her "get-up," is not "official." Now we understand where the first line's doubt really settles. In what sense is the woman "his" if, unlike the car, she is not "official"—does not act according to the decorum of his position? (Should we deduce that the police officer insists on this point from the adjective "petty"?) We can assume that she is married to the policeman (though if not, she would still probably be "his" mistress). But the poem enforces a recognition that what this marriage means in terms of possession or control is more complex than the ownership of a car.

More exactly, "Exercise" distinguishes, not between possessing cars and possessing people, but between areas of experience in which concepts like ownership apply and areas in which they do not. If these areas are essentially separate (as the poem claims), and if poetry works to juxtapose disparate areas of experience (as this poem, in the act of distinguishing them, inevitably does), then the theme of "Exercise" again relates to the dual task to which Williams puts poetry: isolating experience, making the distinctions necessary to its proper perception, yet acknowledging the continuity of all experience. His free verse contributes directly to this aesthetic. The constant length of his stanzas imposes only the mildest order; his highly irregular lines seem to engage experience with perfect directness. The poem discovers—in a casual structure that seems to say, This among other things simply happened—a form which subsumes structure and event into active meaning.

The same theme informs another poem by Williams in which lineation again counterpoints syntax to provide the general prosody. Partly because its subject is poetry, the theme and its aesthetic implications are more overt in "Poem" (105, 39):

POEM

The rose fades
and is renewed again
by its seed, naturally
but where

save in the poem
shall it go
to suffer no diminution
of its splendor

In this poem the continuity of experience is represented by the
seasonal cycle of life. This cycle suggests a number of alterna-
tives to the division and order of the first two lines. For in-
stance, if the poem were primarily about the continuation of
natural cycles, these lines might be combined. Here, where
the object is to interrupt the cycle, Williams separates fall and
rise. The simplest way to interrupt it would be to leave out
the second and third lines and substitute "and" for "but" in
the fourth. But Williams again, as in punctuating "Exercise,"
takes pains to give nature its due. He could also have de-
scribed the rise first—the blooming of the rose—and then
noted that in nature bloom would be followed by decay, and
finally declared that the rose could nevertheless be preserved
in its perfection by art. This preservation would recall the
plucking of order from formless experience in "Exercise."
And yet, though the cycle's negative half may have inspired
him to interrupt it, he acknowledges instead the other half
(decay making way for later bloom) by letting it complete his
account of the whole. He does not so much claim a victory of
immortalizing art over the transience of nature, as establish a
complementary mode of existence for beautiful objects. Fur-
thermore, this order more plausibly illustrates the poet's
procedure—observing the whole cycle, then freezing the rose
at its point of greatest "splendor"—and thus encourages our
participation.
    The third line is separated from the first two to clarify their

imitation of the natural cycle. It is divided from the fourth for
clarity of sense. A comma within line 3—the only punctua-
tion in the poem—isolates "naturally" and so calls attention
to its two meanings: "of course" it is seeds that perpetuate the
cycle; and "in a natural way" as opposed to the poem's pres-
ervation of the individual rose. This apparently trivial pun
proves valuable later on.

Line 4 is the point at which attention turns from nature to
art. It is so short, not to underscore any complex sense, but to
provide the necessary time for the turn. (Compare the short
line in the middle of the first stanza in "Musée des Beaux
Arts.") Turning the poem at the end of its first half, rather
than waiting for the beginning of the second, is a device used
also by Yeats. (Examples are "Memory" and "A Deep-
Sworn Vow.") In "Poem" it serves two complementary pur-
poses. First, it prevents the first half of the idea (nature) from
standing alone, self-contained and unqualified. This is
partly—as often in Yeats—a matter of pace; if the poem were
allowed to close too fully at its mid-point, it might have diffi-
culty getting started again convincingly. Thematically, the
asymmetrical division reinforces the interdependence of na-
ture and art, an interdependence residing both in art's use of
the objects of nature for its materials, and in what may be
thought of as the perfection of nature by art. Second, the divi-
sion does allow the second half to be self-contained. Because
we have already been through the first stanza, and because the
sentence continues across the break, there is no danger that we
will take the idea of art to be divisible from that of nature. But
if art is a matter of order (if only of an order of words distilled
from a chaos of facts which the words name), it is fitting that
the stanza representing art should have a formal symmetry
denied the stanza representing nature. The last stanza, then, is
a neat group of four lines. It is emblematic of the interdepend-
ence of art and nature that this group of four should strike one
as "neat" simply because it repeats, or imitates, the four-line
pattern of the previous stanza dealing with nature. (Again, the
mental set generated by such verse, the impression of dis-

covery, distracts the reader from analogies to conventional quatrains.) These final lines gain additional coherence by consistently alliterating on sibilants, by employing a subtly but distinctively elevated or archaic diction, and by allowing the syntax more continuity than in the relatively choppy first stanza.

The beginning of the fifth line shows another reason for the isolation of line 4, which creates a position of emphasis for the word "save." The preposition means "except" or "unless," and these synonyms will stand for two nuances of tone, both present in "save": "Except" implies that the alternative of art is perpetually available, so that the poem's question seems to celebrate things as they are. "Unless," on the other hand, makes the line a dubiously hopeful interjection in an otherwise elegiac question, "Ubi sunt." Furthermore, prepared by the pun in line 3, the emphasis on "save" also brings out as a secondary meaning its more usual use as a verb—a verb that expresses precisely what the poem does for the rose, a verb that the rest of the stanza paraphrases and defines.

One more effect of lineation in this poem demands attention. If every line must have some special weight of its own, why does "shall it go" deserve a line to itself? The most mechanical answer is that this is an important syntactical member, the predicate of the second clause in the poem's sentence; but the line goes deeper than that. "Shall" connotes both uncertainty (as in "What shall I do?") and the certainty of a future tense referring to an inevitable event ("The dead shall rise"). The ambiguity of "shall" continues that of the preposition "save." To these we might add "naturally" from line 3. This punning technique takes part in the poem's prosody, in that it arises partly from lineation (which emphasizes each of these words) and contributes a kind of lingering doubleness to the poem's movement. As part of the form, it imitates the poem's broader meaning: the double functions of these words provide a simplified and intralinguistic model of words' capacity to give the rose a double existence.

To put it another way, this short line indicates the poem's

most complex and pervasive pun. The poem is concerned with poetry, and in this respect the most important effect of the isolation of line 6 is to stress "go." This apparently simple verb, which would go almost unnoticed as a mere syntactical exigency but for lineation, is in fact a metaphor. The rose cannot literally "go" anywhere, being sessile; and in any case it could not "go" to the poem, which is not a place. (The echo of Waller's "Go, lovely rose" helps to extend the point to all poetry.) Rose and poem are incommensurable. They happen in different universes. "Poem" thus declares itself (and poetry) *not* to be "organic" in the strictest sense. The experience in which Williams allows us to participate is not cultivating roses but writing poems. But by participating in that act we come to understand it as one of metaphor. The "rose" is not a rose, but stands in the same relation to language—a system of other words—as roses do to nature—a system of other things. (The double reference of "rose" reinforces this perception: The rose preserved by the poem is a flower, not the perennial bush that renews itself "by its seed, naturally.") To ask, as the lineation forces us to do, how the rose (or "rose") can "go" to the poem, is to pose the most basic question about language and thus about poetry: What is the relation between words and things? The answer "Poem" gives is metaphor, imitation.

The forms of both these poems are discovered. Their prosody is one of counterpoint between syntax and lineation. Syntax inherently entails "organic" unity, since the thing to be said and the sentences in which it is said develop inseparably as we follow them. Lineation, too, is determined by (as it determines) the sense of the poem it organizes. Though the principle of discovered form can be seen working in nearly every modern poem, and indeed in some sense in every poem, in Williams's work it becomes the primary and almost exclusive determinant of prosody in all its details.

By its choice of subject, "Poem" acknowledges more fully than "Exercise" the *poetic* context of any poem. This raises a question that will occupy us in the next chapter. Where does the poet discover his form? In the material—that is part of the answer. But we can recognize form only when we have a context in which to see it. Despite the rhetoric of spontaneity in some free verse, all forms are to some degree received. Invention—the poet's side of discovery—means finding, not creating out of nothing. Still, one can distinguish forms whose invention emphasizes their resemblance to past poetry, and forms which are presented as arising out of a context of speech. Though the distinction cannot be absolute, we can clarify the latter part of it by examining from another angle Williams's attitude toward the poet's autonomy.

For Williams, prosody begins as individual rhythm: "Clearly from this point of view 'prosody' means a great deal more than the mere mechanics of versification. Prosody means the rhythm of the poet's personal speech as it partakes of the rhythm of a cultural idiom" (95, 306). The theory of organic or discovered form implies an impulse toward individualism or personal authenticity. But in moving from Coleridge through Whitman and Williams, one sees the realm of discovery expanding to include not only the content of a specific poem ("the properties of the material") and the poet's individual imagination, but the whole culture that supplies his language. The differences between English and American idioms begin to be noticed and insisted on at about the time free verse comes into prominence. "Poem" plays on these differences (as does "Exercise" with "get-up"). In the American idiom, "save" is a verb, hardly ever a preposition; and "shall" is less likely to appear as a future tense than as part of a sentence like "What shall I do?" This setting of the American against the British also has something to do with the poem's subject (roses, art against nature) and its diction, the second stanza departing farther from the American idiom than the first. The distinctions may be more historical than geographic; but the two are linked, as the names Old World and New World suggest. "Poem"—and still more "Exercise"—is determined to appear new and American.

According to Arthur E. Christy, distinguishing idioms has been a preoccupation among Americans for some time:

> John Erskine has pointed out that there are even now [1929] diverging language movements in English poetry. The cadence of American speech is no longer that of the English, and since it was from the English models that the best American poets fifty years ago learned the cadence of both their speech and verse, it is not surprising that the American ear today detects a strange, almost foreign note in the fall of the lines of such poets as Tennyson, Lowell, and Longfellow. Americans speak with more directness, with less subtlety and delay. . . . We seem hungry for verse the cadence of which will be native to our ears [25, 212].

This may help to explain why, as Walter Sutton argues, "although the modern movement in the arts was broadly international, the free verse movement in English has been a predominantly American phenomenon" (98, 1-2). Especially interesting in this regard is the testimony of Denise Levertov, an Englishwoman who married an American and came to this country to live. She had read Williams's poems before, but

> what I felt about the poems in those first eight months or so, between my first finding them and my coming to America, and perhaps even after that for a while, was that I literally didn't know how they would sound. I couldn't read them aloud. I couldn't scan them, you know. I didn't understand the rhythmic structure. . . . After I had lived here for a little while, I picked them up again, and I found to my joy that I could read them—and I think it was simply that my ear had gotten used to certain cadences [99, 324].

Williams's insistence on "the American idiom" is especially well known. As Mary Ellen Solt summarizes, "In his emphasis upon the prosodic structure of our speech as the foundation for his personal dialect, Williams has realized that the truly significant styles are those which make use of the organic characteristics of languages: those which do not depend upon 'effects' added by a skillful technician" (95, 313). The opposition is too simple. But all these comments make clear where Williams turned to discover his prosodic forms.

The expansion of discovery to the linguistic culture as a whole has become, especially for American poets, one of the most common defenses against the solipsism that has threatened to isolate the individual poet and poem entirely ever since "authenticity" became a primary aesthetic value. But for others, and especially for British poets, the linguistic culture cannot be divided from the literature it has produced. It is their use of that literary context that will concern us next.

Chapter Six

The Discovery of Meter

METER AS DISCOVERED FORM

William Carlos Williams "discovered" the form of "Exercise" and "Poem" in the very speech that constitutes them. In each poem we seem to grasp the saying and the finding of its form as simultaneous acts. Philip Larkin's "Church Going," on the other hand, a British poem published in 1955, uses iambic pentameter. By no stretch of terminology could it be called free verse. If its form is "discovered," the realm of discovery must be sought not so much in speech—even British speech—as in the tradition of English poetry. Why not simply say that the poem is metrical, and leave it aside? I want to argue that the prosody of such a poem can be fully comprehended only with and through the concept of discovered form; by seeing the poem in this light, we will see as well the connection between a modern metrical poem and free verse.

The first stanza sets out both the iambic pentameter and the poem's idiosyncratic stance toward that meter:

Once I am sure there's nothing going on,

I step inside, letting the door thud shut.

Another church: matting, seats, and stone,

And little books; sprawlings of flowers, cut

For Sunday, brownish now; some brass and stuff

Up at the holy end; the small neat organ

> ˣ ˣ ′   ′ | ˣ ′ |ˣ ′ ˣ | ˣ ′ ˣ
> And a tense, musty, unignorable silence,
>
> ′   ′ | ′   ′   ′ | ′   ′ | ˣ ˣ ′ ′
> Brewed God knows how long. Hatless, I take off
>
> ˣ ′ |ˣ ′ | ˣ ′ | ˣ ′| ˣ ′
> My cycle clips in awkward reverence . . .

The first line is metrically normal, only a common initial in-
version varying the basic pattern. The same inversion follows
the caesura (again a standard position) in the second line,
which ends with a spondee. The third line has only nine syl-
lables; here the caesura disguises a missing slack. This is the
most traditional point (after the first syllable) for a defective
foot; but the technique departs from what has been the most
usual practice since after Wyatt. The fourth line returns to the
pattern of the second, but an unusually late secondary caesura,
creating a strong enjambement, threatens the stability of the
metrical line. These relatively slight disturbances unsettle
one's ear; but the regularity of the next line reestablishes the
norm.

The norm is nearly shattered by the following two lines. I
have scanned the sixth as ending with an iamb and a palim-
bacchius, though it could as well have taken a bacchius and a
trochee. The unfamiliarity of the terms indicates how very
odd the line is metrically. The pair of amphibrachs that termi-
nates the next is almost equally peculiar; the initial rising
ionic, though not too strange in itself, contributes to the
obscuring of the meter. The eighth line, with three spondees
and another ionic, is not much more familiar. The sixth and
seventh, if not the eighth, might well be called incorrect
within a traditional framework.[1] We recognize an underlying
pentameter in them; I shall argue later that that is the final test.
But the actual lines depart about as far from the meter as they
can without destroying it entirely. If the stanza did not end
with another regular line, the poet would have severely
shaken our confidence that we are, and ought to be, hearing
iambic pentameter.

Similarly, while rhymed stanzas are a traditional form, this rhyme scheme is an unfamiliar one: *a b a b c b d c d*. More strikingly, some of the rhymes themselves are not merely slant or assonantal; Larkin manipulates the placement of accent in the rhyming words. (Marianne Moore does the same to silence the rhymes in one stanza of "Bird-Witted." But the precedent is an isolated one, and her meter is itself radically separate from the English tradition.) We deduce that "organ" rhymes with "on" and "stone" only by looking ahead to other stanzas ("font/don't/meant"; "do/too/show"). "Silence" and "reverence," though their terminal phonetic characters are otherwise similar, differ in stress. On the other hand, many of the rhymes are recognizably normal, varying between full ("shut/cut") and slant ("stuff/off"). Both in rhyme and in meter, then, the actual lines alternate regular and irregular realizations of the abstract pattern. To put it in a way that will be helpful later on, the poem approaches and recedes from traditional regularity.

One's first thought might be that such a poem merely represents a logical step in the relaxation of iambic pentameter. This relaxation has been going on at least since Wordsworth, more evidently in Browning and most in Hopkins. Thus, the oddities of this poem's form might be due to a prosodic history which, though it includes the poem, is extrinsic to it. Yet as soon as we take in the whole poem, rather than trying artificially to isolate its prosody, we see that a kind of irony, a consistent doubleness of meaning, pervades it on every level. In examining this doubleness, we begin to see intrinsic reasons for the poem's prosodic uncertainty.

The title provides a telling example in miniature. At least when we return to it after reading the whole poem, it blossoms with ambiguity. Is the "Church" a building, or an institution, or something (like "church service") that includes both? Is "Going" an adjective—describing either the decaying building or the dying institution—or a participle? And if it is a participle, does "Church Going" mean attendance at service, or the speaker's mere tourism ("once I am sure there's nothing going on")? No decision can fully answer these questions. The title includes all the combinations of these meanings. A phrase from a later stanza shows again how many senses Larkin is ready to condense into a few words: "this cross of ground." Again the main alternatives concern the physical and the spiritual. "Ground" refers to both the foundation of the church and the foundation it once provided. "Cross" is simultaneously a symbol associated with the church as an institution, and the concrete shape of the building's ground plan. (Even the reasons for this shape exhibit the same split: Churches were cruciform for both iconographic and architectural reasons, this shape requiring a shorter roof span than would a rectangular building of the same area.) By these ambiguities, Larkin announces that his subject is both the institution on which he meditates and the building that houses and occasions the meditation. And as the "church" is both stone and system, the pentameter line is both verbal rhythm and metrical abstraction. Larkin explores both these relations— and both the connections and dissociations that define them—simultaneously.

The speaker's tone is richly complicated by the same means. His diction veers between the casual ("some brass and stuff") and the reverent ("this cross of ground"), and often combines the two ("Up at the holy end"; "God knows how long"). A line like the first ("Once I am sure there's nothing going on") speaks simultaneously to all kinds of emptiness in the church, and thus implies both his careful and sardonic distance from its traditional functions and his sadness in acknowledging that those functions are disintegrating. His observation of physical details walks the same line: The "sprawlings of flowers, cut / For Sunday"—for a day of every work or a Sabbath—are "brownish now," later in the week or later in history, when no one but a tourist like himself or a "ruin-bibber, randy for antique" would bother to visit the place. Gradually all the world is retreating, like himself, into disbelief—or more than that, as hatred is not so far from love as indifference:

> But superstition, like belief, must die,
> And what remains when disbelief has gone?

For whatever personal and historical reasons, the speaker cannot believe in the church, in the traditional system of religion. Yet in the desolation of "what remains," he misses it badly. The poem's ambiguities contribute to a tone composed in equal parts of amusement, reverence, and sadness, each of them directed almost equally at the church, at the modern world that has no apparent use for it, and at his own complex nostalgia ("Hatless, I take off / My cycle clips in awkward reverence"). He misses religion because it once did what its name says: it tied things together. It linked not only the people whose community it defined, but the phases and events of human life. The walls of stone that housed it

> . . . held unsplit
> So long and equably what since is found
> Only in separation—marriage, and birth,
> And death, and thoughts of these . . .

Isolated from each other, these events lose their transcendental meaning and are reduced to biological habits; yet the church once gave them dignity and significance as parts of a whole:

> A serious house on serious earth it is,
> In whose blent air all our compulsions meet,
> Are recognized, and robed as destinies.

Now, for one like the speaker, "bored, uninformed, knowing the ghostly silt / Dispersed," the only substitute for the church's function is something like the poem itself, gathering up the details ("grass, weedy pavement, brambles, buttress, sky") into a meditation that still returns to the church for its center—as it is bound to do,

> Since someone will forever be surprising
> A hunger in himself to be more serious,
> And gravitating with it to this ground,
> Which, he once heard, was proper to grow wise in,
> If only that so many dead lie round.

That the poem's own unifying meditation seems like a *mere* substitute for lost religion indicates how far Larkin feels himself separated from Matthew Arnold. Still, Arnold's vision of poetry as the heir of religion retains some of its force. "This ground," in the poem's last lines, is not only the church but the poetic substrate on which Larkin raises his building stanza by stanza.

Since the poem's power of feeling is aimed toward the past, the traditional iambic pentameter is a logical prosodic choice. Because of the complexity of that feeling, the poem's rhythm of advance toward and retreat from the meter is equally logical. This logic exceeds any static unity of form and content. In reading the poem we are continually aware of the poet's own awareness of the form; the form is discovered. More, we understand that his use of it is, in Schiller's distinction, not naive but sentimental. He knows the traditional meter, but knows it from outside; he accepts it, but provisionally; he retreats from it, though he can never quite turn his back.

Vers Libéré

Philip Larkin owes perhaps his greatest poetic debt to T. S. Eliot. Eliot's own poems—by quotation, by ceremonious diction, by theme, and by his critical pronouncements—constantly recall earlier poetry. His realm of formal discovery is, like Larkin's, the "tradition" about whose relation to the "individual talent" he wrote his most important essay. But in most of Eliot's poems, the specifically *prosodic* connection with earlier verse is more complicated than in Larkin's "Church Going." Because we hear the tone of older poetry in his lines, our ears are prepared to hear in them the play of slack and accented syllables that has shaped the rhythm of most English verse. We would never think, in reading Eliot, to listen for the syllabic counts of Marianne Moore or "the distribution of 'n' and 'r' sounds" employed by Louis Zukofsky. Yet this familiarity of the primary elements of his verbal rhythms—elements which, unlike Williams, he does

not deliberately divert from their familiar rhythmic pat-
terns—raises a surprisingly difficult question: Should we de-
scribe Eliot's poems as free verse?

Eliot himself clearly realized the impossibility of answering
that question in quite those terms. Instead, he indirectly de-
scribed the main prosodic principle of his own verse in this
way:

> The most interesting verse which has yet been writ-
> ten in our language has been done either by taking a
> very simple form, like the iambic pentameter, and
> constantly withdrawing from it, or taking no form
> at all, and constantly approximating to a very simple
> one. It is this contrast between fixity and flux, this
> unperceived evasion of monotony, which is the very
> life of verse. . . . We may therefore formulate as fol-
> lows: the ghost of some simple metre should lurk
> behind the arras in even the 'freest' verse; to advance
> menacingly as we doze, and withdraw as we rouse.
> Or, freedom is only truly freedom when it appears
> against the background of an artificial limitation [35,
> 33-35].

We must pause a moment for clarification. The whole passage
was probably meant to describe such verse as that of the
Elizabethan dramatists Eliot so admired. If we ignored Eliot's
identification of iambic pentameter as "a very simple form,"
then "taking no form at all, and constantly approximating to
a very simple one" might describe the practice of Williams,
whose forms are discovered in the apparent formlessness of
speech. But Eliot's "simple form" is a traditional metrical
one. Thus it must precede the poem, and in this sense it is
more accurate to say that the poet withdraws from it rather
than that he approaches it.

Characteristically, Eliot gave no name to this delicate proc-
ess of approximating a received form. Graham Hough, how-
ever, points out that the French have done so. On comparing
French and English theories of verse, "we discover at once

that the French distinguish between *vers libre* and *vers libéré*—verse which is born free and verse, so to say, which has been liberated from some pre-existing chains. We have not this distinction in English—partly I suppose because the neat verbal antithesis between *libre* and *libéré* is not available in the English language" (53, 87). J. V. Cunningham helpfully provides a full idea of the resources of what Hough calls *vers libéré*: "in general, the lines of a poem [of this kind] will be partly in standard meter, at times parts of what would be a standard line, or they are felt to be equivalent in some aspect of sound or feeling to a standard line, or they exhibit some marked variation of a standard line, or some other principle of meter is used intermittently and supported and given authority by the presence and recurrence of standard lines" (30, 268). Such a technique of prosodic approximation bears an obvious connection with Eliot's devices of quotation, half-quotation, parody, and allusion, which make his poems resonate with echoes of past poetry.

These iambic echoes have elicited critical attention to Eliot's prosody, generating studies that reflect confusions discussed in Chapter Two. Eliot's own statements encourage some of this misunderstanding. There is, to begin with, the dictum I quoted in my first chapter: "No *vers* is *libre* for the man who wants to do a good job." He expanded on the same theme in his anonymous pamphlet, *Ezra Pound: His Metric and Poetry*: "The freedom of Pound's verse is rather a state of tension due to constant opposition between free and strict. There are not, as a matter of fact, two kinds of verse, the strict and the free; there is only a mastery which comes of being so well trained that form is an instinct and can be adapted to the purpose in hand" (34, 172). These propositions seem at least generally correct. When Eliot remarks that "any verse is called 'free' by people whose ears are not accustomed to it" (34, 167), he summarizes much of what I tried to demonstrate at the beginning of this book. But his insistence that all verse, being hard work, is the same—a position which makes him impatient of distinctions and distinguishing names—sometimes proves a handicap. In the essay in which he describes (but does not name) *vers libéré*, he concludes that "the division between Conservative Verse and *vers libre* does not exist, for there is only good verse, bad verse, and chaos." This surely goes too far. Williams's verse is good, but it is not (or was not when he wrote it) "Conservative," especially if by that word Eliot means "metrical."

More dangerous still is Eliot's chief argument for this conclusion: Free verse, he says, cannot be defined by the absence of meter, because that is impossible. "Any line can be divided into feet and accents. The simpler metres are a repetition of one combination, perhaps a long and a short, or a short and a long syllable, five times repeated. There is, however, no reason why, within the single line, there should be any repetition; why there should not be lines (as there are) divisible only into feet of different types" (35, 32). The tone of prosodic impartiality in these sentences reflects the atmosphere of experimentation to which Eliot contributed—and perhaps an effort to counter mystifications arising from the revolutionary rhetoric of novelty. But his equation of meter with scansion represents poor strategy. Although I think the flaws in his argument are obvious, the principle that Eliot describes here has at least the respectability of an official name. In Classical prosody, "logaoedic verse" mixed different kinds of (quantitative) feet in each line. The mixtures were subject to rule, and only two sorts (two- and three-syllable feet of either rising or falling rhythm) were used in any one poem. Despite this flaw in the analogy, other critics during the free-verse controversy adopted the idea. Richard Aldington seems to be speaking of logaoedic verse when he says that

> the best Greek poets—Alcman, Sappho, Alcaeus, Ibycus, Anacreon even, and the Attic dramatists in their lyric choruses—used a kind of free verse, which is perhaps the finest poetry we have. I am aware that German professors have laboriously worked out the scansion of this poetry; I have com-

pared their scansion with that of certain English free
verse poems and if anything the English poems are
more regular [3, 351].

Summerfield Baldwin allies himself perilously with the
"German professors" by noting that "many of the effusions
of the New Poets, if accented syllables are regarded as long
and unaccented as short, may, with the aid of a table of Greek
metrical feet, be interpreted to contain some very intriguing
rhythms which the authors have all unwittingly utilized in
writing their verses" (11, 60).

To speak of these "intriguing rhythms" as "unwittingly
utilized" is, of course, to parody Eliot's meaning. He praised
Pound's "mastery which comes of being so well trained that
form is an instinct and can be adapted to the purpose in
hand"—a quite different faculty from the naive, unconscious
grace Baldwin seems to extol. Eliot recognized that a prosody
must be shared between poet and reader. Yet his own declara-
tion that "any line can be divided into feet and accents" would
be difficult to distinguish logically from the statements of Al-
dington and Baldwin. All of these ways of thinking about free
verse (or at least *vers libéré*) tend to confuse it with metrical
verse, and to assimilate all verse to the old formula, "metrical
composition."

In the face of the obvious yet subtle alliance between *vers
libéré* and metrical verse, the greatest theoretical temptation is
to reduce the rhythm to its elemental "facts," the accented
and unaccented syllables, and examine them with a kind of
assumed naiveté. (Eliot's insistence that any verse can be
scanned shows a related tendency to ignore prosodic context
in favor of apparently plain and objective fact.) It was to this
method that I traced the fallacy of calling "accentual" all verse
which has accents. Not surprisingly, that is one reduction to
which Eliot's verse has been subjected. Helen Gardner, in her
influential book on the *Four Quartets*, at various points fails to
distinguish scansion from meter, meter from rhythm, and ac-
centual meter from the fact of accent in all English speech. Ul-

timately, these implicit equations contradict each other. Recognizing (though perhaps for the wrong reasons) that Eliot's verse is not metrical in the traditional English sense, Gardner finds its rhythms in speech, and then identifies speech rhythm with accentual meter.[2] One could dismiss this position by remarking that accentualism serves as a last resort for any prosodist uncomfortable with the continually shifting organizations of nonmetrical verse. Yet even Harvey Gross, whose placement of Eliot in a "predominantly metrical context" far exceeds Gardner's in sensitivity and elaboration, returns again and again to accentualism to account for lines not otherwise metrically explainable.

The most extensive and painstaking use of the naive method of prosodic analysis pervades Sister M. Martin Barry's *Analysis of the Prosodic Structure of Selected Poems of T. S. Eliot* (14). Yet her study amounts to an enumeration of various ways in which normal iambic verse can be loosened. To be sure, her system will not take account of such common effects of meter as the promotion and displacement of normal speech accents. It often forces her to overlook regularities that the lines *do* exhibit, as in her scansion of this obvious pentameter from "Gerontion":

$$\overset{\text{x}}{\text{A}}\text{re} \overset{\prime}{\text{forced}} \overset{|}{\text{upon}} \overset{\text{x}}{\text{us}} \overset{\prime}{\text{by}} \overset{|}{\text{our}} \overset{\text{x}}{\text{im}}\overset{\prime}{\text{pudent}} \overset{|}{\text{crimes.}}$$

But on the whole, she too herds Eliot's *vers libéré* as best she can into a metrical corral.

Any failure to distinguish between *vers libéré* and metrical verse would blind us to the difference between Larkin's "Church Going" and most of Eliot's poems. Both would become metrical poets in direct descent from Browning. Yet there is some truth to this. In both poets' work, prosodic form is discovered at least partly within the poetic tradition. But while "Church Going" is a metrical poem, most of Eliot's simply are not. In fact, it is the extreme irregularity of his poems that has tempted critics to reduce rhythm to accent, and themselves to a posture of prosodic innocence. Such a posture not only cripples the analyst, but also places out of reach the most important fact about meter—its systematic conventionality. To seize upon particular conventions— accents, syllable counts, feet—and discard the system within which alone these conventions have any significance, is not to account for a prosody.

If one assumes the relevance of metrical feet to verse like Eliot's, there are two logical ways to extend or loosen the iambic meters, by varying either the kinds of feet or their number. Either method might appear reasonable by itself. The first could be called logaoedic, and one could conceivably argue, with Eliot, in favor of lines "divisible only into feet of different types." Just so, one could cite clearly metrical poems whose lines vary in length. Hardy's stanzas would be a poor example, since the variation is subject to rule; the fourth line of every stanza, for instance, may be a trimeter. Arnold's "Dover Beach," which may indeed have been an important model for Eliot, provides a more convincing precedent. But though Arnold varies the number of iambs in the line (from two to five), he replaces the iambs with other feet only according to familiar principles of substitution, which he applies conservatively. However flexible the accentual-syllabic meter may be, it will not accept both kinds of variation at once in the degree to which Eliot employs them. The concept of the foot has meaning only metrically—that is, within a numerically regular system. When feet vary ad hoc in both number and kind, they lose metrical significance. To calculate, as Barry does, the percentage of iambs in the line and of pentameters in the poem—often less than half in both cases—is not to render the poem metrical. However interesting and useful, statistics are not prosody.

BEYOND THE DISCOVERY OF METER

One cannot account for Eliot's prosody by assimilating it either to accentual or to accentual-syllabic meters in any simple way. Yet in hearing the iambic echoes of Eliot's *vers libéré*, one is forced to agree in part with Harvey Gross's castigation of "early and obviously deaf critics" who "labeled Eliot a 'free-verse poet' and since first misconceptions, like first impressions, doggedly persist, many still think of Eliot as a writer of unmetered verse" (43, 175). We need to see not only the poems' separation from the metrical system, but also their connection with it. The question is how to account for this connection without attempting to apply metrical rules and tests that the poems must fail.

J. V. Cunningham suggests a solution that acknowledges both the nature of meter and Eliot's oblique references to it. In our experience as readers, he says, the iambic pentameter is not so much a matter of rules conformed to or departed from, as a set of "alternate patterns, each of which satisfies the metrical requirements, some more common, some less."

> As we perceive of each sentence, without stopping to analyse it, that it is grammatical or not, so the repetitive perception that this line is metrical or that it is not, that it exemplifies the rules of its meter or that it does not, is the metrical experience. It follows that metrical analysis is irrelevant to poetry; metrical perception is of the essence. You do not have to explain the iambic pentameter; you do have to recognize it [30, 267-68].

(This is why Larkin's poem, despite its peculiarities, is metrical.) To leave the prosodist his proper space, we might argue that metrical analysis can profitably communicate the learned metrical perception. Like any critic, the prosodist tries to make an experience, depending upon implicit knowledge, explicitly intelligible. But Cunningham is surely right to imply that the job of anlaysis is to clarify rather than to replace experience. Morris Halle and Samuel Keyser provide an intriguing example of both the method of prosodic analysis and the boundary at which it must defer to prosodic experience (44). They have created a novel theory of meter by starting from the same analogy as Cunningham: Meter is like grammar. But their search, as structural linguists, for a set of "grammatical" rules for meter encourages them to separate prosody from unruly meaning. This prevents them from explaining, or even considering, how a poem *uses* its meter. Their system excludes the shadowy resemblances on which Eliot's verse depends. Many of his lines fail the test for metricality; yet in them the reader seems to glimpse members of the metrical repertoire. This part of our understanding of the poems needs to be acknowledged.

Our recognition depends on the (for the most part implicitly) systematic conventions of meter. Yet Eliot manipulates the recognition without adopting the system itself. His fundamental technique is to use recognizable *parts* of familiar "alternate patterns." We can see how this works by diagramming some common pentameters, matching them with lines from "The Hollow Men," and underlining the segments of the diagrams that correspond to Eliot's lines [33, 79-82]:

´ × × ´ × ´ × ´ × ´	We are the hollow men
´ × × ´ × ´ × ´ × ´	Trembling with tenderness
´ × × ´ × ´ × ´ × ´	Than a fading star
× ´ × ´ × ´ × ´ × ´	We grope together
´ × × ´ ´ ´ × ´ × ´	In death's dream kingdom
´ × × ´ ´ ´ × ´ × ´	This is the dead land
× ´ × ´ × ´ × ´ × ´	This is cactus land★
× ´ × ´ ‖ ´ × × ´ × ´	Are raised, here they receive
× ´ × ´ × ´ × × ´ ´	And avoid speech
× ´ × ´ × ´ × × ´ ´	The eyes reappear

Though these diagrams *prove* nothing—since what is at issue is not demonstrable prosodic fact but a way of listening to rhythm—they are suggestive. Heard in this way, such fragments are strikingly appropriate to the poem's enactment of disintegration and dissociation. As reminders of what is lost, Eliot mixes with the fragments occasional full pentameters—

★ Despite antithesis to the previous line, metrical resemblance combines with a line break to stress "land."

> The supplication of a dead man's hand
> Under the twinkle of a fading star

—or divides a pentameter between lines:

> Lips that would kiss/Form prayers to broken stone.

Not every line matches so clearly either the pentameter or parts of what would be a pentameter line. Instead, the poem employs a full range of variation, from metrical regularity to apparently random arrangements of stressed and slack syllables. Because the abstract pattern is manifested only intermittently, we must call "The Hollow Men" nonmetrical. It differs radically from "Church Going," and even from "Dover Beach." But because of the poem's deliberate and slightly archaic diction, which makes us listen for each word's lilt; because of the elegiac tone, implying a traditional order that has been lost; and because Eliot thus plays on our own experience at recognizing iambic meter, we attend to the poem's rhythm in a way not entirely separate from that appropriate to metrical verse.

We might be able to summarize all this by saying that Eliot's prosody is one of approximation: *vers libéré*. He controls our rhythmic attention by "advancing" and "retreating" with respect to a metrical norm. He uses not so much meter as our recognition of meter. This is in effect where every prosody must begin—with the rhythmic habits of the reader's ear, which the poem can extend but not ignore. Yet "approximation" implies a prosodic casualness and vagueness that does not answer to our sense of Eliot's verse. And indeed *vers libéré* alone would seem insufficient to do all that we expect of a prosody. The control it makes possible seems at once too minute and too broad. Those lines that represent the farthest departures from meter approach dangerously near randomness. The effect is at times that of a storehouse of metrical bits and pieces gathered from every cranny of prosodic history— an effect which allows the poem to reverberate powerfully, but which seems to subvert the organizing purpose of pros-

ody as Williams's complete abandonment of meter for con-
textually generated structures never does. Furthermore, in
many poems Eliot confuses the technique by constructing
longer lines out of metrically incompatible fragments. "Ger-
ontion" provides examples (33, 29-31). A line like "In de-
praved May, dogwood and chestnut, flowering judas" throws
together the beginnings of three iambic lines. As Cunning-
ham points out, the first part of a line is often a whole pen-
tameter, to which Eliot adds a fragment:

```
 ′    × | ×   ′ | ×   ′ | ×    ′ | × ′
History has many cunning passages, contrived corridors
  . . .
```

```
 ×   ′  | ×  ′ | ×  ′| ×  ′ | ×    ′  ×
In memory only, reconsidered passion. Gives too soon
  . . .
```

Occasionally a line combines these strategies:

```
                        ∧ ′ | ×  ′  | ×   ′ |  ×  ×  ′  | ×
 ×   ′ | ×  ′ | ×    ′ | ×  ′ | ×   ′
In fractured atoms. Gull against the wind, in the windy
  straits . . .
```

Here either the first or the last pair of phrases yields a pen-
tameter; but the two possibilities conflict.

Yet it is just this sort of conscious tension, one pattern
competing with another, that gave Auden such fine rhythmic
control in the contrapuntal prosody of "Musée des Beaux
Arts," or Williams in "Exercise" and "Poem." In fact, pro-
sodic manipulation of syntax and its relation to lineation is
hard to overlook in Eliot's poems. He, too, employs a pros-
ody that comes to seem almost universal in free verse. And
within that system, his approximation to metrical patterns
helps him control lineation with a special precision.

The same increase in control is evident in Eliot's prosodic
use of snytax. In this, despite Eliot's disclaimers, we probably
see the influence of Whitman. I have not said much about
Whitman, since his particular prosody—unlike his liberation

of verse from meter and his insistence on organic form—had little direct bearing on the revolutionary free verse of our century. But in overthrowing the accepted forms of verse in favor of the looser forms of Biblical prose, Whitman relied primarily on syntax to give his lines prosodic coherence.[3] He wrote verse; the organization depends on the line. Since most of his lines are end-stopped, the prosody is not one of counterpoint; the organization is internal to the line. Gay Wilson Allen, in his chapter on Whitman in *American Prosody*, catalogues the various sorts of syntactical parallelism by which the lines establish their structure. These range from the simplest repetitions of words to broad patterns gathering a whole series of lines into shape. When Henry Reed sets out to parody Eliot's late style, he does so by reducing it to a mechanical use of just these devices, and reducing to absurdity Eliot's way of throwing surprises into the rigid structures. The following lines from Reed's "Chard Whitlow" exhibit, besides simple anaphora, Allen's categories of synonymous, climactic, and internal antithetic parallelism (89):

> As we get older we do not get any younger.
> Seasons return, and today I am fifty-five,
> And this time last year I was fifty-four,
> And this time next year I shall be sixty-two.

Eliot's use of these devices is generally more subtle than Whitman's—though the mordancy of Reed's parody suggests that this is not always true. The subtlety can extend to such intricate syntactical puns as this from "Gerontion," in which "issues," melting from a noun into a verb, throws us from the hope of a definite outcome for events back into the despair of the interminable process of history:

> . . . Think now,
> History has many cunning passages, contrived corridors
> And issues, deceives with whispering ambitions . . .

The grammatical shift is prosodic, helping to control our movement through the lines. Both Harvey Gross (43, 85-86)

and Hugh Kenner (61, 124–41) have analyzed this part of
Eliot's technique. It represents one aspect of his prosody. But
Eliot also seems more willing than Whitman (though less
than many other modern writers of free verse) to counter-
point syntax with lineation. When he combines these tech-
niques with the use of metrical fragments, he achieves a strik-
ing degree of delicate rhythmic control.

THE PROSODY OF ELIOT

The full range of Eliot's prosodic strategies is evident in the
Four Quartets, and "Burnt Norton" will provide the examples
we need. In speaking of "The Hollow Men," I have already
discussed Eliot's simplest use of metrical fragments. The fol-
lowing passage shows more fully how his manipulation of
our awareness of meter organizes our temporal experience
(33, 180):

> Words move, music moves
> Only in time; but that which is only living
> Can only die. Words, after speech, reach
> Into the silence. Only by the form, the pattern,
> Can words or music reach
> The stillness, as a Chinese jar still
> Moves perpetually in its stillness.
> Not the stillness of the violin, while the note lasts,
> Not that only, but the co-existence,
> Or say that the end precedes the beginning,
> And the end and the beginning were always there
> Before the beginning and after the end,
> And all is always now. Words strain,
> Crack and sometimes break, under the burden,
> Under the tension, slip, slide, perish,
> Decay with imprecision, will not stay in place,
> Will not stay still . . .

Part of the rhythmic effect here derives from repetitions of
"words" and "only." The noun recurs to keep before us the

object of meditation. (If we accept Hugh Kenner's thesis that
what speaks the best of Eliot's poetry is not so much its
human author or his persona as the language itself, "words"
may name the meditation's subject as well [61, 293-94].)
"Only" distills the whole *method* of the meditation—
rigorously excluding specious possibilities, seizing on the es-
sentials that remain. Besides these, a few lesser parallelisms
provide local control: single repetitions of "music" and
"reach," plays on "still(ness)" and "beginning" and "end,"
and the anaphora on "will not stay."

Aside from these intermittent rhythms of sense and syntax,
the passage achieves almost its entire prosodic control by
modulating among metrical approximations. The second line
approaches closest to a regular pentameter:

Only in time; but that which is only living.

The next line

Can only die. Words, after speech, reach

terminates in a defective foot that removes it farther from the
metrical norm. The same is true of the sixth

The stillness, as a Chinese jar still

in which we readily identify the missing syllable as "is"; its
elimination establishes the pun on "still" which runs through
the next few lines. The thirteenth line pushes the same metri-
cal variation still farther by ending with two defective feet:

And all is always now. Words strain.

The line is not a metrical pentameter, and the passage has not
prepared us to hear a tetrameter. It is possible to speak of "de-
fective feet" in this line only because of the recognizable mod-
ifications of pentameters earlier in the passage, which have

prepared us to listen in that way. This line recalls them just when it returns us to the opening "Words move" with "Words strain."

Our ears are no more prepared to hear a hexameter than a tetrameter. Thus the sixteenth line

Decay with imprecision, will not stay in place

seems rather to break into two quasi-metrical fragments. Other lines are similarly divided. Caesurae strongly interrupt the first four, and the fourth

Into the silence. Only by the form, the pattern

like lines from "Gerontion," adds a fragment to a regular pentameter. The end of the passage shows how the metricality of the fragments can control meaning most directly. It is Eliot's evocation of meter that makes us shift stresses in the repeated phrases of the final two lines:

. . .will not stay in place,

Will not stay still.

This shift clarifies the tone, which modulates from a kind of impatient fatalism back to the passionate and determined reasoning that spondees have suggested throughout the passage.

Interspersed with these modulations, two alternative rhythmic techniques set off and emphasize the metrical resemblances. The passage opens with a self-contained progression that might remind us of Williams's "Exercise." "Words move" establishes the spondaic motif; "music moves" inserts a slack, and "Only in time" adds another. The decreasing density of stress can suggest a relaxation, though this effect is lessened by the firm pentameter that includes the last phrase. Later on, a longer run of looser rhythms provides a second departure from metrical approximation. In the

eighth line, the habits already built up encourage us to pro-
mote syllables unstressed in speech

<pre>
      ˆ , | x   , | x   (,) | x   (,) |x ,
</pre>
Not the stillness of the violin, while the note lasts,

but the line strains these habitual compensations toward their
limits. The next, with its ambiguous opening and low density
of stress, passes those limits: "Not that only, but the co-exist-
ence." Over the next three lines, the rhythms relax more and
more, control passing to syntax and repetitions of "begin-
ning" and "end." The twelfth line approaches, if anything, an
anapestic norm:

<pre>
     x , |x x , | x   x , |x x ,
</pre>
Before the beginning and after the end.

But the next, starting with three clear iambs, reestablishes the
mode of metrical resemblance. At the same time, it brings us
from abstract speculation (a digression signalled by the syn-
tactical impertinence of the previous three lines) back to the
concrete experience of "words" that "strain."

In other passages, syntax contributes proportionally more
to rhythmic control, and metrical approximation recedes into
the background. The beginning of the poem is typical, if
extreme:

> Time present and time past
> Are both perhaps present in time future,
> And time future contained in time past.
> If all time is eternally present
> All time is unredeemable.

Here, little more than the simple density of stress allies the
lines with meter—though the passage ends with a recogniza-
ble tetrameter.

Instead, Eliot produces a conviction of inevitability by
avoiding periphrasis, repeating each term whenever the rea-
soning calls for it. The repetitions, replacing metrical certain-
ties, may remind us of Whitman; but syntactical parallelism is

less important than the circular logic of incantation. The doublet, "past/future," first distributed to the ends of the opening lines, is recapitulated chiasmically in the third. (Chiasmus is perhaps Eliot's most pervasive trope in such passages.) Aside from this relatively incidental pattern, our attention is captured and directed by the three occurrences of "present," threaded through the seven of "time." The middle lines simply toll out "time . . . time . . . time." But while these insistent repetitions imitate the certainty of logic, it is the variations that embody the logic itself. The first line ("time . . . present . . . time") unfolds into the last two. There Eliot inserts "eternally"—a word that summarizes the whole passage by gathering up past, future, and present—and replaces "past" with "unredeemable." This word—the longest, and the one whose possibly promoted final syllable first suggests a metrical sense of rhythm—is the conclusion toward which the previous lines drive, and which their insistence is meant to reinforce. It is the very circularity of the logic of time that makes it "unredeemable."

Eliot's longer lines usually have less metrical feel to them than his shorter *vers libérés*. Often they tend to be end-stopped, like Whitman's, and then syntactical controls take over:

> At the still point of the turning world. Neither flesh nor
>   fleshless;
> Neither from nor towards; at the still point, there the
>   dance is,
> But neither arrest nor movement . . .

Here the suspensions and ambiguities by which Eliot controls our movement are performed by uncertain or absent reference (both subject and predicate are missing from these sentences, unless we settle on "There is") and the incantatory or quasi-liturgical repetition of paired opposites. Yet this pattern, too, becomes one element in a larger rhythm, balanced in a kind of ebb and flow with counterpointed syntax and lineation. A few lines later, we find this:

The inner freedom from the practical desire,

(another end-stopped, yet syntactically open line)

The release from action and suffering, release from the
   inner

("inner" we have already heard, but the structure of antithesis
tells us that now it will modify a noun, which stands against
"freedom")

And the outer compulsion, yet surrounded

(we are given the noun, but the surprising addition of "and
outer" has thrown us a little off-balance—an instability which
the enjambement uses to push us onward)

By a grace of sense, a white light still and moving . . .

At the end, when the sentence has arrived at the "grace" and
"light" toward which we now see it as having pressed, its
conclusiveness is reinforced by the echo of a pentameter.

Harvey Gross, analyzing Eliot's poems under the aegis of
Donald Davie's "syntax like music," summarizes the peculiar
effect the verse can have:

> Like music these lines affect the reader by move-
> ment of sound; they offer the structure of feeling
> without denoting the human problems that gave rise
> to the feelings. Music is the art which deals with
> emotion in the abstract; the joy or agony we feel
> when we listen to music is never an explicit joy or
> agony. By suppressing the logical forms of gram-
> mar and blurring the edges of experience, Eliot
> achieves a quasi-musical effect. Syntax, the very
> form of thought, becomes a means for conveying
> feeling; we respond to Eliot's lines without fully
> comprehending them. Rhythm tends to become au-
> tonomous and separate itself from the rational struc-
> ture of the poem [43, 86].

But if Eliot's prosody is "abstract," it is simultaneously perfectly concrete. He creates the awareness of movement—of rhythm in the broadest sense—without giving awareness anything stable to focus or depend on. The effect is less to separate rhythm from "the rational structure of the poem" than to erase any possible distinction between form and content, prosody and thought. If syntax is "the very form of thought," a prosodic form based on it is inevitably organic.

But Gross's description must also be expanded to include *all* of Eliot's rhythmic techniques: counterpoint and metrical approximation as well as syntactical manipulation. *Vers libéré* is not in itself a prosody. Yet Eliot controls our temporal experience, now holding us back, now pushing us onward, carefully managing where our attention settles, how fast it shifts, and what it combines. Prosody does not merely reflect, but in a sense *is* the meaning of the poem. It would be difficult to give this prosody any general name. The fluctuating experience of recognition and half-recognition, continually alerting us to our relation to the traditions of poetry and the conventions of syntax, is too absolutely inseparable from the poem itself to be identified by an isolating name. Attention to the rhythms of sound—the normal effect of prosody—becomes one with attention to the rhythms of thought.

Chapter Seven

Free Verse and Poetry

What kind of poetics demands a nonmetrical prosody? Why do some poems need to be realized in free verse? Prosody and poetry mutually determine each other's character. Prosody makes sense, and is worth studying, only because it contributes systematically to the total meaning of a poem. A prosodic form that arises by being discovered within the content it shapes can be described only in its natural habitat, the poem that subsumes both. What new poetry required the prosodic novelty of free verse?

A knowledgeable observer in 1912 could have supplied one simple answer: Imagism. In that year, Ezra Pound, along with H. D. and Richard Aldington,

> agreed upon the three principles following:
> 1. Direct treatment of the "thing" whether subjective or objective.
> 2. To use absolutely no word that does not contribute to the presentation.
> 3. As regarding rhythm: to compose in the sequence of the musical phrase, not in sequence of a metronome [87, 3].

These "tenets of Imagism" announced the beginning of modernist poetry. The third one officially certified the birth of free verse. Like the others, it has to be understood as part of a self-conscious revolution. Hence its adversary tone; hence also the bald equation it implies between meter and "metronomic" (mechanically regular) rhythm, and its simplistic assumption that "musical" rhythm dispenses with conventional constraints. Once a place for free verse had been fought clear by such propaganda, the reformers—at least those commanding Pound's learning and taste—could afford to stop renouncing other prosodic alternatives. Still, free verse arrived on the scene in company with a "New Poetry" most obviously represented by Imagism.

Did free verse merely accompany Imagism, or did it result inevitably from the Imagist doctrine? The three tenets declare a new contract between poet and reader; the third constitutes its prosodic article. Do the three imply each other, or did the Imagists embrace free verse only for its novelty? At first sight, the third tenet seems almost an afterthought. The others concern the stuff of which a poetics is made: the nature of poetry and its relation to the world. The second, stressing the key word "presentation," recalls the pictorial foundation of the New Poetry. The first establishes both the content of the Image, which it refuses to limit, and the general method of "treating" it. Yet the third refers narrowly to the technicalities of verse structure.

One can quickly dispose of this spurious distinction between levels of theoretical discourse. Pound, for instance, allows no such separation: "I believe in technique as the test of a man's sincerity" (87, 9). Since prosody belongs to meaning, a change in ways of meaning will require a change in prosody. But why specifically free verse? If we try to trace this choice directly to the second tenet's demand for conciseness—seeing free verse as the result of excising extraneous words from metrical lines—we will be forced to condemn it as an expedient resorted to by versifiers who could not match their predecessors' skill. Tempting as many opponents of free verse found this explanation, we can deduce a better one from the system of Imagist doctrine as a whole.[1]

Near the heart of Imagism lies the belief that, as Pound puts it, "the poetic fact pre-exists" (87, 54). What the poet "presents" is an Image. Pound first defined the Image as "that which presents an intellectual and emotional complex in an instant of time" (87, 4). This "complex" ("in the technical sense employed by the newer psychologists") exists before

the poet "treats" it, or embodies it in language. Some of Im-
agism's lesser followers took this to mean that a poem simply
names a collection of objects: the willow tree by the boat-slip
in the blue river. But properly understood, the "poetic fact" is
not a " 'thing' " in this naive sense; we must not forget
Pound's quotation marks. Before the poet "treats" it, the
"poetic fact" does not so much exist as occur. Pound soon re-
placed his earlier, static definition of the Image with new for-
mulations that emphasized its movement (86, 36; 63, 56ff.).
As Hugh Kenner points out, the Image becomes a plot in the
Aristotelian sense—the imitation of an action (63, 57).

Even in general terms, what makes the "poetic fact" poetic
is not its content but what we might call its shape. If the
Image consists (as it frequently does) of a collection of objects,
the "poetic fact" is not the objects themselves but the rela-
tions that bind them into a whole. Eliot describes how the
poet discovers his images: "When a poet's mind is perfectly
equipped for its work, it is constantly amalgamating disparate
experience; the ordinary man's experience is chaotic, irregu-
lar, fragmentary. The latter falls in love, or reads Spinoza, and
these two experiences have nothing to do with each other, or
with the noise of the typewriter or the smell of cooking; in the
mind of the poet these experiences are always forming new
wholes"(35, 64). (Eliot offers a characteristic ambiguity about
agency: The poet amalgamates experiences, yet they form
wholes as if by themselves. About what used to be called "in-
spiration," the early modernists were deeply reticent.) The
dynamic relations among things constitute the Image, and the
"poetic fact" is above all a process, objects *acting* on one
another.

When the poet renders this action of things into language,
he constructs an interaction of words to represent it. The
poem, looking both ways, informs both things and words.
Indeed, the action of words in a poem is called form, and
prosody is its aspect most accessible to analysis. To put this as
an analogy: What the Image does among things, form does
among words. The Imagist poem imitates nature.[2] Just as the
poet must find the "poetic fact" in nature ("whether subjec-

tive or objective"), so he imitates that discovery in his form. Imagist theory, then, entails discovered form as an essential part of its mimetic project.

Yet we have already seen that discovered form need not mean free verse. We can find a more intimate connection by examining the function of the poet, who mediates between the unwritten "poetic fact" and the reader. The poet's job, say the first two Imagist tenets, is to "treat" or "present" his material. How he communicates this process to the reader—the nature of "presentation"—remains mysterious. But it becomes less so if we look beyond the tiny original Imagist clique to the wider circle of early modernists, as I have already done in quoting Eliot. Arthur Mizener puts his finger on the center of the mystery. The "ordering form" of Eliot's verse, he says, "derives immediately from Ezra Pound's imagism":

> Pound's imagism is only one manifestation of an almost mystical theory of perception which is one of the remarkable phenomena of our time. From James's "represent" through Joyce's "epiphanies" and Mr. Eliot's "objective correlative" to Hemingway's "the way it was," our writers have been dominated by a belief that every pattern of feelings has its pattern of objects and events, so that if the writer can set down the pattern of objects in exactly the right relations, without irrelevances or distortions, they will evoke in the reader the pattern of feelings [76, 20].

Thus Mizener identifies what connects poet and reader, though he cannot explain it. But we can align this "theory of perception" with the relation between poet and "poetic fact." Again mimesis will provide the connection.

In Mizener's list we find the most famous (or infamous) name for this belief in correspondence that underlies modernist poetry: Eliot's "objective correlative." But though Mizener speaks of the objective correlative as though it stood outside the poem, Eliot calls it "the only way of expressing emotion in the form of art" (35, 48).[3] This requires some

"pattern" in the poem itself that will "evoke in the reader the
pattern of feelings." In the most simple-minded version of
Imagism, the poet merely sets down names and hopes that the
reader will imagine the objects they stand for. However, if the
"poetic fact" comprises above all a temporal shape, its cor-
relative within the poem must also be a process: generally,
form; and specifically, rhythm. As the poet imitates, by his
form, the shape or process of the "poetic fact," so form helps
the reader to imitate the process within himself. These two
imitations meet in the shared discovery of form. Pound's "ab-
solute rhythm," then, is the most fundamental objective cor-
relative: "I believe in an 'absolute rhythm,' a rhythm, that is,
in poetry which corresponds exactly to the emotion or shade
of emotion to be expressed" (87, 9). And since "symmetrical
forms" so rarely provide this correspondence, we have at last
the mark that identifies free verse as a child of Imagism.

"Absolute rhythm" precipitates two elements of modernist
theory that seem to oppose each other; immediately after
defining it, Pound makes one of them explicit: "A man's
rhythm must be interpretative, it will be, therefore, in the
end, his own, uncounterfeiting, uncounterfeitable." Juxtapos-
ing these sentences, Pound seems to identify "absolute
rhythm" with "a man's rhythm." The connection recalls
those attitudes of Williams that I described at the end of my
fifth chapter: Prosody begins as individual rhythm, and both
derives from and verifies the poet's autonomy or authenticity.
If technique is the test of a man's sincerity, prosodic technique
tests his rhythmic authenticity and confirms the truth of what
Eliot calls his "auditory imagination." This doctrine follows
almost automatically from modernism's Romantic heritage
(from which the rhetoric of revolution, and even some real
distinctions, should not distract us). It surfaces, in the writings
of defenders of the New Poetry and of free verse, in demands
for novelty and individualism. Taken to an extreme, it yields
Edward Storer's claim, which I have discussed before, that
"Every man's free verse is different."

Yet if this extreme is implicit in modernist poetics, so is its opposite. Eliot's most central essay, "Tradition and the Individual Talent," devotes itself to expositing an "impersonal theory of poetry." In searching for "the poetic fact," the poet must avoid especially those "irrelevances and distortions" that arise from his own personality. For this reason, as Eliot says, "the more perfect the artist, the more completely separate in him will be the man who suffers and the mind which creates" (35, 41). Answering Wordsworth, he declares that "poetry is not a turning loose of emotion, but an escape from emotion; it is not the expression of personality, but an escape from personality" (35, 43).[4] This "impersonality" of modern poetry has inspired the same accusations of coldness and egocentric obfuscation as the insistence on personal authenticity that it balances. But what matters is the balance itself. On the one hand, the poet's personal preferences must not blind him to the "poetic fact" which claims his primary responsibility. It comes to him with its own innate form; he must not allow a predilection for sonnets, for example, to distort that form. Yet on the other hand it is only the poet who can perceive and so realize that innate form; this is the primary function of "the mind which creates." On questions of prosody, he must consult himself; not his personal self—rather, his "ear." Eliot's "auditory imagination" and Pound's "absolute rhythm" entail the whole doubleness of this capacity; the poet's "ear" derives authority from both impersonality and authenticity, and for Eliot the two imply each other.

The charge that Eliot's theory makes the poet "cold" is obviated by the tremendous emotional difficulty he acknowledges in achieving the necessary "impersonality." After equating poetry with the escape from emotion and personality, he immediately adds, "But, of course, only those who have personality and emotions know what it means to want to escape from these things." The poet effects this arduous detachment by confronting something larger than himself. Eliot identifies this larger thing as "tradition." Like Pound, he is careful to distinguish between the vital use of a poetic tradition and the mere parroting of conventional sentiments in conventional phrases jammed into conventional forms. "We shall often find," he says of the poet, "that not only the best, but the most individual parts of his work may be those in which the dead poets, his ancestors, assert their immortality most vigorously" (35, 38). Tradition—the right use of convention—becomes a means toward individuality. By maintaining the tension between these poles, the poet keeps his balance and carries intact to the reader the "poetic fact."

To the extent that free verse derives logically from Imagism, we have accounted for its invention. But this historical explanation suffers from a pair of flaws. In the first place, Imagism was an extremely short-lived movement. Officially, it existed long enough to produce a couple of anthologies. Even before the end of the Great War, its inventor, Pound, had moved beyond it. (Amy Lowell took it over; Pound branded the new movement "Amygism.") Though one can certainly argue that modernist poetry began with Imagism, it would be wrong to call all modern poetry Imagist. Yet though free verse has not held the kind of exclusive sway it briefly enjoyed, it has remained high on the list of prosodic alternatives of which poets avail themselves. If we insist on identifying it too closely with Imagism, this continuity becomes hard to account for. In the second place, I have argued at several points that the roots of free verse reach back much farther than 1912. Nonmetrical prosodies predate the Old Testament; even as a movement, free verse must be traced at least to Coleridge's definition of "organic form." These two difficulties can help us to refine our view of the poetic history of free verse.

If by "free verse" we mean not only verse using a nonmetrical prosody but verse set self-consciously against traditional meters, then we will seek its origins in the poets of the nineteenth century, not in the older literature some of them enlisted in their reforms. The impulse toward prosodic renewal manifested itself throughout that century, beginning before Coleridge's "Christabel." But this renewal followed two patterns. Browning (and Victorian England's metrical virtuosi, Tennyson and Swinburne, and, for that matter, Hopkins) chose a different way from Whitman. The poet could loosen accentual-syllabic meter, increase its flexibility, even eliminate one of its elements and refresh his rhythms by returning to the old accentual meter. Or he could abandon meter entirely, in favor of still older principles of verbal order. If we remember that the distinction is more convenient than precise, we might call these the British and American ways of revitalizing prosody and poetry.

Just as the free-verse movement grew from these two roots, so it quickly developed two parallel branches. Lumping together all the modernists partly falsifies the historical picture. They found more than one point of equilibrium for the tension I traced in Pound's and Eliot's theory. In the last two chapters we have examined two versions of the poet's discovery of form, and of his relation to "poetic fact." We might say that while Eliot stresses tradition, Williams stresses the individual talent. But since both poets (like all poets) must balance the two, we could distinguish more usefully between the constraining contexts within and against which each defines himself and discovers his poetry. Eliot confronts his poetic heritage; Williams confronts "the American idiom," the speech of his contemporary culture. The directions chosen by Eliot and Williams continue those indicated by Browning and Whitman.

These two confrontations represent the most common realms in which modern poets discover their forms, though not the only possible ones. Poets as early as George Herbert realized some semantic uses for typography, and the advent of both typewriters and visually irregular free verse encouraged many poets to experiment with the look of their poems, and to demand a new kind of control over the print-shop. E. E. Cummings manipulated typography in ways we must call prosodic, discovering form in literal shape (43, 122-26). For most poets, however, to turn so radically from the spoken or liter-

ary word to the specifically printed page was to avoid but not
solve the problems of poetic language that most concerned
them. I will return to those problems after looking a little
farther ahead in poetic history.

Both Williams and Eliot began very near Imagism. Pound
made himself the mentor of both, and it would be hard to
mistake the connections. But they developed the Imagist idea
in different ways. Though both used free verse, they refined it
in different ways. Since prosodic distinctions relate to broader
issues of poetics, we should not be surprised to find Williams
noting a real split between what he conceived of as aesthetic
necessity and the poetic style that Eliot's great success made
temporarily universal. "His reader's expectations of
'poetry,' " Hugh Kenner remarks, "are not part of Williams'
poetic as they were of Eliot's" (60, xvi). *The Waste Land*

> implies a poetic. It offers to say—to show—how
> poetry must be written in our time. If nothing will
> grow in our stone civilization, if no dance is stepped
> to the sound of horns and motors, then the poet's re-
> course is to go back, to recover the old words, use
> again the old stones, learn the lost meanings: which
> means, for an American, rejoin the European past.
> ... What goaded Williams into much cerebration . . .
> was the presence and celebrity of *The Waste Land*.
> His response to *The Waste Land* was immediate and
> visceral: it was going *back*, in his opinion; it was
> even (he did not avoid melodramatic terms) an act of
> betrayal [60, 63-66].

Unlike the opponents of free verse, however, Williams did
not accuse Eliot of undermining civilization—quite the oppo-
site. Instead, he saw his ex-compatriot as obstructing neces-
sary and inevitable progress. Both poets wanted, like Pound,
to "make it new"; but Eliot would have stressed the first of
those words, Williams the last.

Later on, modern poetry underwent further changes and

developments. Many poets rebelled against the impersonality Imagism had imposed—the peculiar *silence* of the Imagist poem—and began to refine again on the possibilities of discursive statement. But Imagism always mattered more as a nexus of propaganda than as a body of poetry, and as such it has continued to influence the poetry that grew away from it. Its chief continuing effect has been to foster a pervasive belief in discovered form. That principle, in turn, though it does not require free verse, encourages it.

When we try to discern in later verse the two main styles of nonmetrical prosody initiated by Eliot and Williams (and derived in part from Browning, Whitman, and others), we must not lose sight of the qualifications these oppositions demand. Both poetry and speech necessarily form the background of any poem. I have noted that Whitman exerted some influence on Eliot; such cross-fertilizations between styles never cease. Furthermore, in turning to *vers libéré* Eliot had in part the same motive as Williams (and Browning and Wordsworth): to obtain greater apparent accuracy in imitating speech. And Williams continually refers to past poetry, whether by subject (as in "Poem") or diction or formal allusion (as in the terza rima opening of "The Yachts"). The differences, though important, are matters of degree and of rhetorical strategy.

Indeed, all I have said here concerns the free verse written by those poets who invented it around the time of the Great War, and those who refined it over the next five or six decades. We habitually group them all as "modernists," despite their differences; and we distinguish them more and more certainly from the poets who are our contemporaries. The further elaboration of various kinds of modernism, and the possibility of real departure from that diverse moment, will be the subject in the next chapter. But in one way or another all poets since the early modernists have depended on them. It will be useful to consider once more the causes of their revolution before speculating about more recent developments.

In the first chapter I gave a broadly inclusive definition of poetry: A poem is the language of an act of attention. Though

we have examined instances of this attention, I have not tried
to explain an act that the poet himself cannot fully com-
prehend. But at least in part the poem pays its attention to
language; it is this aspect of the definition that I have tried to
explicate.

The definition is deliberately ambiguous. On the one hand,
the poem itself is made of words, or rather of language; it is a
semiological artifact. This artifact is organized and made to
mean, not only by the conventions that make all acts of lan-
guage mean, but by additional semiological systems that de-
pend on further, specialized conventions. Many of these addi-
tional systems fall into the category of prosody. Prosodic
form is an essential, semantic element of poetic language. But
on the other hand, the poem imitates speech and, ultimately,
the dynamics of thought codified (or, perhaps, imitated) by
speech—"the 'thing' whether subjective or objective." The
relation between these two languages—the imitating one and
the one imitated—has varied considerably in different phases
of poetic history. At times the imitation seems, to both poets
and readers, gratifyingly close. Poetic language offers the poet
a powerfully precise medium in which to present "the poetic
fact"; it provides the reader with a precise guide for his own
replication of the poet's experience of that "fact." At other
times, one party to this contract or community begins to
sense a disappointing and even alarming disparity between
the "fact" and the inherited poetic language available for pre-
senting it. The supplementary conventions that define *poetic*
language seem to petrify it; the language grows too rigid to
keep faith with what the poet has for it to present. Almost al-
ways the poet senses this disparity—the linguistic component
of what Eliot called "the dissociation of sensibility"—before
the reader, who may strongly resist the reforms that the poet
undertakes as a result. But as Pound remarks, "What the ex-
pert is tired of today the public will be tired of tomorrow"
(87, 5).

Poetic language does not become imprecise by falling into
conventionality, though the urge toward revolution may lead

poets to simplify the case in that way: Poetic language, like any language, depends on conventions. Rather, poets begin for some reason to change the way they see and feel—the "act of attention" undergoes a kind of cultural shift—and so to glimpse new "poetic facts." In the failure of poetic language to adjust to these new materials, the culprit is some pervasive and habitual misuse of traditional conventions. The sense of disparity between old poetic language and new "poetic fact" naturally calls attention to the complex relation between the contemporary poet and the tradition he inherits from his predecessors. The shrewder theorists in each revolution acknowledge this complexity. Thus Pound advises poets: "Neither is surface imitation of much avail, for imitation is, indeed, of use only in so far as it connotes a closer observation, or an attempt closely to study certain forces through their effects" (87, 93). And Eliot, in his Introduction to Pound's collected *Literary Essays*, draws the same distinction: "As for the reputations that he has attacked, we must recall the reaction against the Augustan Age initiated by the Lake Poets. Any pioneer of a revolution in poetry—and Mr. Pound is more responsible for the XXth Century revolution in poetry than is any other individual—is sure to attack some venerated names. For the real point of attack is the idolatry of a great artist by unintelligent critics, and his imitation by uninspired practitioners" (87, xi).

Eliot's citation of "the Lake Poets"—itself expressing a belief in useful precedent—serves to remind us that Wordsworth and Coleridge conducted a reform parallel in many ways to that which again became necessary a hundred years later. Coleridge described the deterioration of poetic language that denied it ideal precision and encouraged revolution:

> Sometimes . . . I have attempted to illustrate the present state of our language, in its relation to literature, by a press-room of larger and smaller stereotype pieces, which . . . it requires but an ordinary portion of ingenuity to vary indefinitely, and

yet still produce something, which, if *not* sense, will
be so like it as to do as well. Perhaps better; for it
spares the reader the trouble of thinking; prevents
vacancy, while it indulges indolence; and secures the
memory from all danger of an intellectual plethora
[26, ɪ, 25-26].

Though Coleridge traces this state of affairs to a steady de-
cline since "the days of Chaucer and Gower" (similarly, Eliot
localizes the "dissociation of sensibility" in the seventeenth
century), we may suspect instead that the precision of poetic
language deteriorates periodically, impeaching its fidelity to
"the poetic fact"; the cycle ends in revolution.

These revolutions, as well as the problem that inspires
them, follow similar courses. At least this has been true of the
last two. But the solution can be formulated in two ways,
with somewhat different effects on practice. The poet dis-
satisfied with the present state of poetic language always
moves forward by moving back; but he can return either to
earlier and more precise literary models, or to speech as he
hears it. Coleridge remarked on this difference between his
own and Wordsworth's reactions to the problem:

When, therefore, Mr. Wordsworth adds, "accord-
ingly, such a language" (meaning, as before, the lan-
guage of rustic life purified from provincialism)
"arising out of repeated experience and regular feel-
ings, is a more permanent, and a far more philosoph-
ical language, than that which is frequently substi-
tuted for it by poets, who think they are conferring
honor upon themselves and their art in proportion
as they indulge in arbitrary and capricious habits of
expression:" it may be answered, that the language,
which he has in view, can be attributed to rustics
with no greater right, than the style of Hooker or
Bacon to Tom Brown or Sir Roger L'Estrange [26,
ɪɪ, 40].

The distinction Coleridge draws between himself and Wordsworth provides a clear analogy to the one I have drawn in these last chapters. Williams's "American idiom" bears only a distant similarity to the language of English rustics before the Industrial Revolution, and Eliot's literary models are not Coleridge's. But the underlying distinction has remained.

Yet behind the differences in Eliot's and Williams's poetry stands one similarity that linked nearly all the early modernists: They chose free verse as the prosodic method by which to revive poetic language by reestablishing its precision. It worked because it combined the new and the old. As the virulence of attacks on free verse demonstrates, it represented a drastic revision of the contract between poet and reader. By revising the contract, free verse helped "make it new," restoring to the reader "the trouble of thinking" and the "danger of an intellectual plethora." A petrified poetic language cannot mean—is *"not* sense," as Coleridge puts it—because it deadens the reader's attention. Yet the revision would have failed if free verse had not also provided renewed contact with much older, fundamental conventions of poetic language. Because it was new, free verse could newly arouse the reader's attention to the temporal experience of the poem; because it was old, because it depended on sufficiently permanent conventions, it could control that experience. Free verse revitalized poetic language, in short, precisely because it was a prosody.

Chapter Eight

Some Contemporaries

Any attempt to account for contemporary poetry in a way that will remain convincing after twenty years—or perhaps two—is foredoomed. As Eliot's perception of the Tradition implies, even our assumptions about the relative importance of various first-generation modernists are subject to revision as new poets with new acts of attention change the total shape of poetic history. Yet the poets of our own time have extended the paths begun half a century ago, which we can follow, and may have found new ones, whose direction we can try to deduce.

Before turning to specific poems, we might extrapolate tentatively the double curve I have been examining in modernist prosody. At least as representatives of prosodic innovation, Williams and Eliot still seem to preside over most of the discoveries, experiments, and achievements of the poets who have come after them.

In terms of the fashions of influence, it seems clear that Eliot's star was declining by mid-century, as Williams's rose. Eliot has few notable *direct* followers at present. But if we think of Eliot, not as exercising his former hegemony, but as representing a tendency, we begin to see his shadow touching fully half of contemporary poetry. Through W. H. Auden to Robert Lowell, Richard Wilbur, Howard Nemerov, and many others runs a tradition of flexible, eclectic, and skillful metrical verse that Eliot did much to perpetuate by showing how it could embody modern themes and voices. After Theodore Roethke (whose free-verse poems owe more to Auden's than to those of Eliot himself), few major poets have adopted Eliot's intricate ambivalence to meter. For the most part the poets on this side of the field have returned to meter—though with the subtle awareness of alternatives which we saw in Larkin's "Church Going."[1] Though I have argued that this awareness derives from the historical fact of free verse (and from the historical situation that gave rise to free verse), metrical contemporary poetry does not come within my subject. I will say no more about it, except that my neglect indicates only the scope of this book, not any deficiency in the power or originality of the poetry.

Since mid-century, a definite new lineage of poets has emerged, holding new allegiances. As Hilton Kramer recently remarked, reviewing *The Little Magazine in America* by Mary Kinzie and Elliott Anderson, the rebellion of the avant-garde in the fifties "often consisted of little more than pitting the 'new' Pound-Williams team against the old Eliot-Pound team of the more academic quarterlies" (66, 32). The next major figure in the new group is Charles Olson, born in 1910, who looked back more or less equally to Pound and to Williams. Olson's verse has excited the emulation of many poets, and his "Projective Verse" has exerted more influence than any essay by a poet since the first modernist generation. That it is no more comprehensible in technical terms than Williams's notes on prosody has not made it less important as a manifesto, and a closer look at it helps to define the dominant style of the last two decades.

The essay is famous for its almost mystical insistence on "the breath" as the fundamental principle of poetry. Olson emphasizes "breath" as physical; it is the force behind the voice, something *heard* in the poem. As a principle, its area of competence is prosodic; it specifically governs lineation: "the HEART, by way of the BREATH, to the LINE" (4, 390). In part, this theory returns us to T. S. Omond in 1908, or even beyond: "It is not uninteresting to ask what determines the length of verse-lines. Oliver Wendell Holmes thought it was lung-power—that Spenser must have habitually breathed more slowly than Prior, 'Anacreon' more quickly than Homer" (81, 119). In 1950, Olson seems to have revived the

old idea of "cadence," which Amy Lowell had defined thirty
years earlier as a "rhythmic curve . . . corresponding roughly
to the necessity of breathing" (73, 141). Even earlier, at the
end of the first World War, Mary Hall Leonard summarized
another foray in the same direction, and its answer: "Fletcher
tells us . . . that 'each line of a poem, however many or few its
stresses, represents a single breath.' To this Professor Alden
has caustically replied that the lines of free verse are absolutely
irregular and that '*vers libre* must be unhygienic if it develops
such irregular breathing' " (68, 23). Clearly this part of Ol-
son's idea is neither new nor immune to ridicule. But to dis-
miss it so reductively is to miss his point. We can find out the
basis of his contentions by investigating a more serious mis-
understanding, encouraged less by his theory than by his ex-
pression of it.

Denise Levertov stands close to Olson in her alliance with
Williams, and one of her poems will shortly provide us with
an example of recent work in this tradition. But her sympathy
enables her to point out the risk involved in one way of read-
ing Olson's essay. In an interview, Walter Sutton asks her,

> *You think then that the rhythm of the inner voice controls*
> *the rhythm of the poem?*
> Absolutely, the rhythm of the inner voice. And I
> think that the breath idea is taken by a lot of young
> poets to mean the rhythm of the outer voice. They
> take that in conjunction with Williams' insistence
> upon the American idiom, and they produce poems
> which are purely documentary [99, 332].

Olson himself knew better. While the "young poets" of
whom Levertov speaks concentrate on the second half of Ol-
son's formula—the motivation and determination of the line
by the breath—he seems to have meant attention to fall
equally on the first half: the breath is the path by which "the
HEART" finds its way into the line. This is surely a matter of
"the inner voice." (It remains a prosodic principle, and so de-
clares an intimate relation of prosody to feeling and thus to

meaning.) Though his emphasis can be misleading, Olson, with his interest in etymology (4, 398), clearly meant "the breath" to stand for a complex of voice and spirit: "the breath has a double meaning which latin had not yet lost" (4, 393).

In this sense, "the breath" represents, for Olson, the great lesson taught by Williams. It identifies the poem with the poet's individual voice, and finally with his individual being. This is not the solipsism it might appear, but the same poetic method manifested in the air of continual spontaneous improvisation we feel in Williams's carefully crafted poems. The poet's work, Williams insists throughout *Paterson*, must become indistinguishable from his life (104, 116); thus it becomes authentic. (Eliot, on the contrary, sought authenticity through intelligent relation to the Tradition, and thus through an "impersonal theory of poetry," and thus at last through separation of "the man who suffers and the mind which creates.") By imitating the poet's personal speech, the poem becomes universal. In *Paterson*, Williams meant to show forth the city so that it would "be as itself, locally, and so like every other place in the world" (104, viii). The same transfiguration is achieved by the poet who represents his own voice exactly in the poem. This is how, and why, in Olson's terms, the breath mediates between the heart and the line.

Everything in the poem, then, must contribute to the presentation of the poet's voice, and so to his and the poem's authenticity. Despite his approval of Cummings, Olson does not bless the typewriter because it would allow him to create the visual prosody discussed by Harvey Gross (43, 122-26). Rather, he wants its spatial manipulations to stand for temporal ones with a new precision. "For the first time the poet has the stave and the bar a musician has had. For the first time he can, without the convention of rime and meter, record the listening he has done to his own speech and by that one act indicate how he would want any reader, silently or otherwise, to voice his work" (4, 393). The poet's "own speech" clearly stands against metrical "convention." Yet within another page Olson has acknowledged that this will require a new set of conventions. His own device of a vergule in the midst of a line (to represent "a pause so light it hardly separates the words") would need to become a convention in order to do its job. Otherwise it would remain idiosyncratic—individual and therefore authentic, perhaps, but uncommunicative. Olson is no solipsist. He defines the poem as "energy transferred from where the poet got it . . . by way of the poem itself to, all the way over to, the reader" (4, 387). His theory holds far aloof from hermetically private aestheticism. But the same awkwardness remains which led Edward Storer to protest too loudly that "every man's free verse is different," and which made partly absurd the hope of Whitman, unique as he was, to found a new school of poets. It is a modern version of the old paradox of using a traditionally sanctioned mode—poetry itself—as the vehicle for individual expression.[2] For Eliot, the paradox resolves itself in a right understanding of Tradition. For Olson and other followers of Williams—and, as we saw earlier, for Williams himself—it becomes the dilemma of having to establish new conventions based on old ones, without relinquishing a pioneering, individual, anticonventional stance. Like Williams, Olson had the public visibility to manage it, if only because of "Projective Verse." But it is worth noting that few of his followers have used his midline vergule; nor have many imitated the three-line stanza of his and their original master.

Olson's insistence on the authenticity of the poet's voice, his refusal to separate prosody from feeling, and the link that Levertov rightly discerns with Williams's "American idiom," all place "Projective Verse" in the long line of manifestoes for "organic form." The phrase Olson attributes to Robert Creeley, "Form is never more than an extension of content" (4, 387), is as direct and even simplistic a statement of that doctrine as one could wish. Here Olson's other formula, parallel to that which connects heart and breath and line, comes into play: "the HEAD, by way of the EAR, to the SYLLABLE" (4, 390). His paragraphs on the syllable (4, 388-89) are among the most obscure in the essay. But he firmly stresses the syllable as the atom of *sound*, and as the root of prosody:

"It is the king and pin of versification, what rules and holds together the lines, the larger forms, of a poem. . . . It is by their syllables that words justapose in beauty, by these particles of sound as clearly as by the sense of the words which they compose" (4, 388). But though his emphasis may again be misleading (as always in such an essay, it is governed more by didactic considerations than by any strong sense of theoretical balance), he does not ignore the function of syllables as units of sense.[3] In fact, the syllable is the common denominator of sound and sense in language, in which prosody and meaning most clearly and most "organically" unite.

Olson opens the way for a theoretical connection between prosody and diction. One of his younger colleagues (Creeley) quotes another (Robert Duncan) as making just such a connection: "That the breath-blood circulation be gaind," he requires, "an *interjection*! the levels of the passions and inspiration in *phrases*; second, that focus be gaind a *substantive*, the level of vision; and third, the complex of muscular gains that are included in taking hold and balancing, *verbs*, but more, the *movement of the language*, the *level* of the ear, the hand, and the foot. All these incorporated in *measure*" (4, 411). This becomes a real difficulty in the analysis of contemporary prosody. The revolutions of the modernists in prosody and in the wider field of poetics were, as I tried to show in the last chapter, coordinate; but there is seldom any difficulty in distinguishing them for purposes of analysis. By the time these lessons have been learned by a second or third generation of poets, the welding of prosody to diction or syntax has made them almost inseparable. This is perhaps another way of saying that after the achievements of a revolution have been assimilated, they coalesce into an identifiable period style. Once we have examined Williams's innovations—his further development of the principles of discovered form—Olson's essay gives us the clues we need to understand the predominant style of the decades following the Second World War.

Denise Levertov seems less entangled than Olson in the dilemma of anticonventional rhetoric. Though she emphasizes,

like others, her own confrontation with the world as immedi-
ately perceived, she does not seem to insist on any absolute
novelty or uniqueness of vision. One reason for her flexibility
may lie in the relative lateness of her conversion to this
American style after an English childhood, and her idiosyn-
cratic education in libraries rather than schools. But more
fundamental may be her historical position. Born in 1923, she
has done her mature work well after Williams had not only
broken the ground but settled it and (after the publication of
Paterson I in 1946) gotten it recognized as habitable. Williams
is part of the tradition for her. In this sense she is typical of
younger poets of the late fifties and sixties and early seventies,
though she is more successful than many others at adopting
and developing Williams's prosodic methods. Here is a short
poem from her 1964 volume, whose title, *O Taste and See*,
summarizes the ethos of a whole kind of poetry (69):

THE GROUND-MIST

In hollows of the land
in faults and valleys
                the white fog
bruised
        by blue shadows
a mirage of lakes

and in the human
faults and depths
                silences
floating
between night and daybreak
illusion and substance.

But is illusion
so repeated, known
                each dawn,
silence
        suspended in the
mind's shadow

always, not substance
of a sort?
   the white
bruised
   ground-mist the mirage
of a true lake.

Levertov's prosodic debt to both Williams and Pound strikes the eye even before we take in the sense, in the short lines distributed across the page. Yet the eye is not the relevant judge. As we read, and particularly as we listen to the poem, we begin to understand the thrust of Olson's emphasis on the syllable. Even more than in Williams, we are asked to hear every atom of sound, to appreciate it for its own shading before it takes its place in any larger context. Thus a line like "and in the human"—can one imagine such a line in Eliot, let alone in Milton?—justifies its separate existence first of all by the tiny resonance of "n" and of schwa "a" and "e," and perhaps "i." The invitation to such minute attention, the extreme fragmentation of the flow of language and isolation of the fragments, paradoxically reinforces our sense of the poem as speech. Its background is not space (on the page or in the landscape) but silence, into which words and phrases are dropped one by one. (Despite the importance of lineation and its independence from syntactical pattern, it is not quite right to speak of enjambement in this poem; nothing can "run over" where the language is so discontinuous.) Sense in language inheres in the connections among units of sound; because Levertov sequesters them from one another with such severity, we do not arrive at the sense of her poem without first vividly experiencing its sound, which we automatically associate, in all its hesitations, with a speaking voice. Lacking another name to assign this voice to, we hear it as the poet's own.

Of course we do not stop with sound; the voice *says* something. But the importance of the delay may be emphasized by considering the poem's relation to the modernist tradition. Its departure from that tradition is only a matter of degree, and far from complete. It takes its impulse, like any Imagist poem, from something concretely seen. The ground-mist functions as an objective correlative: the set of facts outside the poem that serves as the poet's occasion of feeling and, presented in language, as the reader's. Here, as often in Imagism, the facts are visual details. But partly because of the insistence on sound and the voice by the fragmentation of sense, the reader's attention focuses less on the visual image than on its "treatment," or on the poet in the act of "treating" it. As compared with earlier Imagist verse, "The Ground-Mist" shows us the poet turning inward, toward the movement of her own "heart, by way of the breath, to the line" in all its miniature delicacy.

I suggested earlier that "enjambement" is not an appropriate term for this poem because it does not so much counterpoint syntax as explode it. As both William E. Baker and Donald Davie have pointed out, modernist poetry shows a strong tendency to subvert syntax or dispose of it altogether (10; 31). (Williams, one ought to note, often uses the sentence masterfully as a central structural principle in his poems.) But in "The Ground-Mist," something more complicated happens; and when we gather the sound of the voice toward a meaning, Levertov's syntactical manipulations prove to be our most important guides. It might be said that she does to syntax what Eliot does to meter, approaching and receding from it in such a way as to control our movement through the poem. Certainly its effect is prosodic in that sense. We begin with a "sentence"—the first half of the poem, lines 1 to 12— which carefully avoids any predicate. After two prepositional phrases, "the white fog" (line 3) has the feel of a subject. But after three more lines of modifying description, we arrive not at any action on the part of the fog but at a stanza break. When the next stanza begins, "and" signals something like a new "clause"; "in the human . . ." establishes a construction parallel to the beginning. We never do get a finite verb (the use of "floating" instead of "float" demonstrates Levertov's care in avoiding syntactical commitment), and by the time we arrive at the full stop after "substance" we understand that the only action is to be the grammatical making-parallel of the fog and the human silences. This substitution of metaphorical juxtaposition for syntactical sequence is typically Imagistic, and seems a task that calls, by the principle of organic form, for language made static by fragmentation.

Yet Levertov—like Williams—is too interested in mutability to be satisfied with that stillness; and what follows, beginning with the discursive "But," is less typical. It is a sentence, indeed a rhetorical question that the poet addresses to herself. Though this question contains two concrete terms, "dawn" and "shadow," the second is made metaphorical by the adjective "mind's," and the first clearly enlists the metaphor established by the first half of the poem. The sentence concerns "the human/faults and depths" more than those of "the land." Levertov has made a definite movement from vehicle to tenor, and from observation of the landscape to introspection. That movement is made possible by the metaphor-by-juxtaposition of the first twelve lines. But it is made actual by the shift to syntactical cogency. The landscape is static, says the poem; it is the mind that moves, and in moving connects and completes things in a way that can be represented by syntax. This shift is a startling one; the poem's structure begins to imply that the demands of Image and of thought are contradictory. The poem cannot afford to abandon either, yet is restless among the accepted methods of reconciling them. Understandably, then, the last four lines delicately refuse to confirm or deny the shift. Their syntactical status is ambiguous: Do they constitute a separate "sentence," like the first, or are we to understand a second question-mark at the end? We cannot be sure whether the return to landscape is accompanied by a return to the stillness of nonsyntactical language, or if the landscape is now allowed to share the motion that the mind has achieved by turning on its own axis.

One way to understand the issues raised by this question is to say that the poem hovers between acceptance and rejection of the traditional modernist function of the objective correlative. On the one hand, the emphasis on sound and the voice, implying the poet's authenticity, reinforces the faith in individual sensory experience that the book's title, *O Taste and See*, so forcefully endorses. That faith is also implicit in the poem's generally concrete language. A striving toward concreteness in language—the subordination of other linguistic processes to that of naming—is one corollary of the doctrine of the objective correlative. On the other hand, the poem's method partly conflicts with the purpose of that doctrine, which is finally to facilitate communication between poet and reader by giving them a common ground. If sense in language inheres in the connections among units of sound, meaning in experience inheres in the connections among units of perception, not simply in the units themselves. The poem's linguistic fragmentation, besides emphasizing sound, tends also to atomize experience into isolated glimpses, and thus to fragment the meaning that the reader is asked to share. The danger, of course, is that "energy," as Olson puts it, will cease to be transferrable "to, all the way over to, the reader."

Levertov raises, in a subtle way, problems that grow severe in the work of many contemporary poets: contradictions between the objective correlative and the primacy of the individual voice; between faith in sensory experience and recognition of the mind or self as the maker of meanings. The poem seems almost ready to leap to some new unity of thought and image, of subject and object, and thus of poet and reader. Yet it remains anchored in modernist tradition. These problems were implicit in modernist theory from the beginning, and help to account for the disparity between theory and practice in the careers of Pound, Eliot, and Williams. By the sixties, they begin to grow acute. "The Ground-Mist" explores, with some discomfort, the limits of modernism. But it also shows that the prosodic methods of Williams, modified by a new flexibility in the use of syntax, will serve to control the rhythm of a poem that begins tentatively to depart from Imagist assumptions.

In John Berryman's primary work, *The Dream Songs*, almost the only echo we hear of Williams's prosody is a regular stanza combining with irregular lines. On the one hand, each of the 385 poems, with only the slightest variation, consists of three six-line stanzas. This uniformity functions partly as it does in many short poems by Williams, gesturing casually toward imposed order without accepting the kind implied by regular stanzas in Hardy or Tennyson or Keats. The stanza provides a firm ground from which rhythmic attention can easily turn to more specific and more variable rhythmic structures. But the repetition of the basic form in poem after poem throughout a long book allies the whole more closely with cycles of sonnets (of which Berryman also wrote a collection) than with Williams's individually discovered forms. The three long beats of this stanzaic drum finally become a kind of "meter" governing the whole of *The Dream Songs*.

On the other hand, there is no question of a meter in the more usual sense. The stanzas' lines can vary between extremes like these:[4]

> who even more obviously than the increasingly fanatical
> Americans (31)

> eyes? (21)

> said:—We are using our own skins for wallpaper and we
> cannot win. (53)

Such lines are clearly "free" in the ordinary sense.

But the case is more complex, and has less to do with Williams, than this initial impression suggests. Robert Pinsky, in pursuit of a different point, makes the experiment of rearranging one line (85, 28):

> Often he reckons, in the dawn, them up (29)

toward an order that stands much closer to the norms of speech:

> Often he reckons them up in the dawn.

Whatever other comparisons one can adduce between these versions, and whatever other motives for the inversion one can infer, the prosodic difference is obvious: Berryman's line is an iambic pentameter, and Pinsky's is not. It is as if Berryman had, like the most bumbling of beginning metrists, shuffled the words until he got them stuffed into the pattern. The rhythmic appropriateness of the line in context, and the many other evidences of Berryman's technical skill, assure us that this "incompetence" is deliberate; but   remains to be explained. Here Pinsky's own main point offers a useful analogy, or something more than analogy.

Pinsky's reading of Berryman, as an example of *The Situation of Poetry* since 1959, emphasizes Berryman's "strategies for retaining or recovering the elevation of Victorian diction" (58, 26). His diction is outlandishly mixed. Bits of "baby-talk" and "minstrel-talk," to use Pinsky's classifications, jostle against words, inversions, and sentiments more nearly "Victorian" or "late-Romantic." Though the slang provides an ironic context, Berryman does not parody Victorian poetry; "it is precisely only the context that is ironic" (85, 25). What this context serves not to mock but to justify is "the kind of language that . . . has tended to be driven out of modern poetry by various pressures: the pressure toward evocative physical description as being the most essentially poetic use of language; the pressure towards idiomatic, spoken discourse" (85, 25).

In part, then, Berryman's diction rebels against Williams's "American idiom," though their motives do not differ absolutely. Both poets aim at a poetry that affirms the authenticity of feeling. To this end, however, Berryman reclaims an old "style which annoys or embarrasses him, but which for some tasks he needs—needs more or less for its original, affirmative, purposes" (85, 36-37). Williams's affirmation is the writing of the poem itself. Even when his impulse is "blocked," he instructs himself, "Make a song out of that: concretely" (104, 62). But the feelings that Berryman needs to present concern guilt, frustration, regret, remorse—feelings which draw the poet obsessively into his own past, and which he may control by turning to the more public past of an elegiac tradition. Yet he distrusts that tradition as artificial, or finds it closed to him. "Verse itself, or natural description itself, threatens to embody a false affirmation or grace, betraying the absolute loss which is the poet's subject" (85, 38). The loss is partly one of order; and indeed Pinsky extends Samuel Hynes's characterization of Hardy to all of "poetic modernism": it is "the ¡nguage of lost order" (85, 34).

The tensions implicit in all this—tensions between the order of verse and a felt loss of order, between artifice and authenticity, between a traditional form of expression and the pressure of individual feeling—ally Berryman more closely with Eliot than with Williams. The diction bears little resemblance to Eliot's, of course. But just as the fragmentation of meter in "The Hollow Men" coincides with that poem's vision of the death of old, hardly replaceable orders, so a similar theme of loss leads Berryman into prosodic methods of which Eliot is the original master.

It is not simply that Berryman mixes metrical and nonmetrical lines as he mixes dictions—though nonmetrical lines often coincide with the entry of a new and slangier voice. More, like Eliot's verse, the Dream Songs approach and recede from metricality. Often they begin metrically. Of the first 77 Dream Songs (first published separately), more than two-thirds open with a probable or definite iambic pentameter. Many of the definite ones are more or less end-stopped and are inverted or peculiar in syntax or diction, in such ways as to suggest that Berryman primed the pump of each Dream with a sort of metrical fantasy. It is hard for the reader to imagine a line like "Bats have no bankers and they do not drink" (63) as anything but the first one written in that poem. This hypothesis—though it is only that—makes us see the poet as starting with the almost prelinguistic fascination of metrical rhythm, rather than with ideas or even feelings. That impression in turn assures us that Berryman has, in Keats's phrase, no "palpable design upon us," no axe to grind, no

"message," but only an obsession to work out from his very
nerves and tendons. The frequent metrical openings, in light
of the discovered or "free" lines that follow, help to guaran-
tee, not subvert, our sense of the poems' authenticity.
Through meter, Berryman meets head-on the suspicion of ar-
tificiality that could attach to the very act of verse.

This is a use to which Eliot did not put *vers libéré*. But the
similarity of method emerges in many passages. The last
stanza of the remarkable twenty-ninth Dream Song shows
how the Eliotic technique can be adapted. Following highly
irregular lines in the previous two stanzas, the third begins
with three firm pentameters:

> But never did Henry, as he thought he did,
> end anyone and hacks her body up
> and hide the pieces, where they may be found.

The sentence is cast as a denial of guilt. It sounds with the
dignity of beleaguered innocence. The solidity of the meter,
the slightly archaic inversion with which the first line begins,
and an energetic anapest in the second foot, all contribute to
this effect. But in the second line the ungrammatical "hacks"
introduces a fantasy which flowers peculiarly from a declara-
tion of innocence; the image is almost specific enough to deny
the denial. Henry is guiltless in action, but not in imagination.
The result of this mixture of dignity and remorse is a kind of
grief; nothing Henry can do, no careful purity of behavior,
can save him.

So frustrating a tension between opposed emotions must
lead to some violent break, and the next line enacts one:

> He knows; he went over everyone, & nobody's missing.

The absurdity of Henry's obsessive self-reassurance ("He
knows"), of the idea of going over "everyone," and of asking
the guilty party (Henry's imagination, in which, surely, he
"went over everyone") to bear witness to innocence, all push
the line toward a kind of hysterical vaudeville. For this sudden
shift in the balance of tone, Berryman breaks the pentameter,

filling out its five stresses with a metrically impossible fifteen
syllables. In the next line, he catches himself up; the pentame-
ter reasserts some control of hysteria. Yet the inversion main-
tains the vaudeville:

Often he reckons, in the dawn, them up.

"Often" and "in the dawn" give to the grief implied by the
first three lines a new edge of pathos. But the very inversion
that creates the pentameter and its return to a more dignified
stability also undercuts this carefully retrieved balance. Henry
has not escaped from his emotional labyrinth. The last line
acknowledges his imprisonment with a kind of exhaustion.
The pentameter cannot complete itself; Henry can only reiter-
ate that "nobody's missing," adding one more to this stanza's
crowd of temporal and personal absolutes ("never," "every-
one," "nobody"):

Nobody is ever missing.

No one is missing in his tallying imagination. But in ac-
tuality—"in the dawn"—no one must ever be allowed near,
lest Henry "hacks her body up."

Berryman's diction, through the tortuous justifications de-
scribed by Pinsky, achieves a special liberty and range of feel-
ing. But the flexibility of tone that draws those feelings to-
gether into a complex self—a self, "Henry" or Berryman,
comprising many voices—depends just as immediately on a
subtle means of rhythmic control. Indeed, the diction and the
prosody work in close concert. Berryman found his means of
control in Eliot's modulated *vers libéré*. Distinct as his aim is
from Eliot's oracular or didactic impersonality, Berryman
stands among contemporaries as the most direct descendant
of Eliot's kind of prosodic modernism.

The prosodic practice of John Ashbery is not especially dif-
ficult to describe in general terms. As in most modern free
verse, particular lineations are "organically" determined by
local context, depending especially on the semantic and

rhythmic effects of enjambement. In his longer poems, how-
ever—I will take as my example "Self-Portrait in a Convex
Mirror,"[5] a poem a hundred lines longer than *The Waste
Land*—Ashbery needs some broader principles of control.
The poem's language is full of reminiscences of Eliot, particu-
larly of the *Four Quartets*: A casual prose diction ("perhaps,"
"On the surface of it," "it will be hard for you/To get to sleep
tonight, at least until late") alternates with passages of
metaphor—

> Mere forgetfulness cannot remove it
> Nor wishing bring it back, as long as it remains
> The white precipitate of its dream
> In the climate of sighs flung across our world,
> A cloth over a birdcage (321-25)

—and passages of metaphysical abstraction used with almost
the tautology of logic:

> . . . "Play" is something else;
> It exists, in a society specifically
> Organized as a demonstration of itself. (423-25)

Often these dictions are combined:

> And we realize this only at a point where they lapse
> Like a wave breaking on a rock, giving up
> Its shape in a gesture which expresses that shape.
>   (198-200)

The last line of "Self-Portrait" feels almost like a quotation
from "Burnt Norton": "Of remembrance, whispers out of
time." Not surprisingly, then, Eliot offers the closest
analogies to Ashbery's prosodic methods. While Berryman
adapted Eliot's earlier strategy of *vers libéré*, Ashbery wields
instead the more embracing principles of the *Quartets*, which
include *vers libéré* among several systems, modulation among
which determines the poem's largest rhythms.
    One can isolate at least three basic sorts of variation that

control the reader's temporal experience of "Self-Portrait."
First and most familiarly, Ashbery varies the contrapuntal re-
lation of syntax and lineation between extremes of enjambe-
ment and coincidence. Within a large section or verse
paragraph, such as the second (100–150), the points of coin-
cidence—end-stopped lines—mark out phases in the general
movement. The progression in length among these phases
clearly indicates the movement of the paragraph as a whole:
We begin with three lines, then six, then fifteen; two shorter
periods of five and three lines hover at the peak; and a long
run of nineteen lines fulfills the whole gesture. Each phase so
defined is itself divided into sentences, whose junctures fall
within and are partially overridden by the lines. On the other
hand, consecutive phases are joined together by syntactical
parallelisms that resonate across the "borders" established by
end-stopped lines:

> . . . I see in this only the chaos
> Of your round mirror which organizes everything
> Around the polestar of your eyes which are empty,
> Know nothing, dream but reveal nothing.
> I feel the carousel starting slowly . . . (120-24)

Both the various divisions and the continuities support, re-
flect, and embody turns in the argument and in the inflection
of the voice. As a method, all of this is familiar from such
examples as the fifth section of "Burnt Norton."

Second, within completely enjambed passages (such as the
first forty-five lines, 151-196, of section III), Ashbery varies
the emphasis of enjambement between *rejet* and *contre-rejet*,
that is, between the suspended last word of a line and the
revealed first word. When the last word is stressed, the en-
jambement is weakened and our movement through the pas-
sage is slowed, as though by punctuation; when the unre-
solved end of a line forces us on more quickly, our attention
presses on the beginning of the next. A kind of controlled im-
balance results, creating an almost continual sense of dis-

covery. We feel the poem's (or the poet's) attention shifting,
cogently, from moment to moment. The effect is difficult to
analyze without quoting a long passage, but the first sentence
of section III gives some impression of the possible rhythmic
flexibility:

> Tomorrow is easy, but today is uncharted,
> Desolate, reluctant as any landscape
> To yield what are laws of perspective
> After all only to the painter's deep
> Mistrust, a weak instrument though
> Necessary. . . . (151-56)

The four balanced stresses of the first line isolate it as a propo-
sition to be expanded; "Desolate" carries that line's energy
(with its syntax) over into the next, and prepares us for the
initial stress three lines later on "Mistrust." In between, "per-
spective" takes enough stress to slow the sentence; but the
construction, "yields what are laws of perspective," demands
completion strongly enough to counteract the deceleration
and create a certain rhythmic tension. This too prepares the
way for "Mistrust," which, as a metonymy for the painter's
aroused attention, centers the meaning of the whole passage.
In sentences like this, the perfect impossibility of separating
Ashbery's syntax from his prosody becomes most striking.

Finally, and most generally, one can say something about
the length of Ashbery's lines. For a variety of reasons—
diction, enjambement, familiarity with the atomistic lines of
poets like Levertov—I find myself continually thinking of
Ashbery's lines as very long. Many are indeed long, and their
length has much to do with their flexibility of statement and
diction. But mechanical examination reveals an interesting
continuity. Though even the average length of lines varies
from one section to another (there is certainly no syllabic or
accentual meter), the variation is surprisingly narrow. It runs
from just over nine to just under twelve syllables; and this is
the range of variation exhibited by normal iambic pentame-

ters. I have said before that statistics are not prosody. But
when one adds to this persistence the many evident pentame-
ters in the poem, especially near its end, one begins to feel an
affinity between the lines of "Self-Portrait" and the standard
English line—if only, crudely, in the sheer amount of lan-
guage each will sustain. Here one might see the last, most dis-
tant refinement of Eliot's approximations of meter. In any
case, our general sense of the lines' length takes its place in the
whole prosodic effect of the poem.

But this description, at most, gives certain hints about the
process of reading the poem. It seems not to draw very near
to what the poem itself says, and the view of prosody I have
put forward in this book leads one to expect always an inti-
mate connection of prosody with meaning. Yet I would like
to argue that such a description of Ashbery's rhythmic con-
trol over our process of reading engages the essence of his
meaning. The argument must be circuitous. What is new in
Ashbery's work, what distinguishes him more sharply than
either Levertov or Berryman from traditional modernism, is
not the prosody itself but its central position in the poem. To
see this, we must for once start from the other end, from
theme.

"Self-Portrait in a Convex Mirror" confronts two ques-
tions: First, what is the self? What does it mean to be a self?
And second, what is a work of art? The poem presents both
an ethics and an aesthetics (and, in the process, an epistemol-
ogy). The two are united in that the speaker meditates on
selfhood while standing before (or rather remembering) Par-
migiano's strange self-portrait, and with its aid. This unity is
finally the poem's main contention. Beginning from aes-
thetics, the reasoning would proceed in this way: To isolate
something, to put a frame around it, is to make it into a fiction
or work of art. The painting itself, so accurate as to fool the
eye and yet distorted, is the most obvious instance, though
one also thinks of "found" art and, more to the point, of the
assumptions about art in Levertov's title, *O Taste and See*. Iso-

lated by "our moment of attention," which is the "room" of whatever "soul" we perceive (43-46), any moment, any "Today"

> . . . has that special, lapidary
> Todayness that the sunlight reproduces
> Faithfully in casting twig-shadows on blithe
> Sidewalks. (379-82)

For this part of the argument, Ashbery need only turn to the familiar language of Imagism.

The next stage unfolds from the first: that to be aware of something—to give it "room" in "our moment of attention"—is to isolate it. In particular, "This otherness, this/ 'Not-being-us' is all there is to look at/In the mirror" (475-77). We examine our selves in the context of the society that forms them, in the mirrors that others present to us, and especially in works of art. To examine or be aware of one's self, then, is to isolate it, and so to make it into a work of art. The self, as it can be known to us or to others, is a fiction (though no more "unreal" than any other; only the attentive isolation called imagination can make something fully real to us). Any self-description is a self-portrait.

Much as I have simplified the poem's argument, it is clear that in its course Ashbery must question certain common distinctions. The self, first of all, collapses into art, as does all of life or nature as known. "Collapses" may be the wrong word, since this distinction, like others in the poem, is not so much destroyed as set partially aside. Like any metaphysics since Kant, the one implied by "Self-Portrait" acknowledges its own lack of logical closure; it does not claim to account for everything.

> But what is this universe the porch of
> As it veers in and out, back and forth,
> Refusing to surround us and still the only
> Thing we can see? (342-45)

The oversimplification, then, is mine, not Ashbery's. But when he recognizes the separateness of art from life by saying of the museum, "You can't live there" (398), the context encourages us to take "there" as referring equally to "today," the present in which the painting, like anything else we attend to, takes its place.

A second distinction assailed by the poem is the philosophical one between subject and object. Again the painting provides the clearest example. In the course of the poem the portrait is addressed by Parmigiano's name, painting and painter are fused, and the space of the painting easily melts into the space of the studio where it was painted and which it reflects. Both spaces become the one in which Ashbery sees the painting, a unity aided by the fact that he is remembering or imagining it. Furthermore, while examining himself in the painting which is a mirror ("you could be fooled for a moment/Before you realize the reflection/Isn't yours" [233-35]), the speaker continually confuses or unites his own self and face and soul with Parmigiano's.

Here one might recall Levertov's "The Ground-Mist," which seemed ready to make the leap to a similar unity of subject and object but turned away uncertainly at the end. Stevens's "Valley Candle," with its deliberate equation of imagined ("subjective") and actual ("objective") experience, comes more compellingly to mind. The comparison suggests that Harold Bloom and others may be correct in finding Ashbery's main source in Stevens. If this is the case, then the revaluation of the early modernists which I mentioned as a possibility at the beginning of this chapter is already under way.

One more such connection needs to be made. If Ashbery's poem implies a theory of the self and of art, it also implies a theory of criticism—as Ashbery, himself an art critic, writing about a painting, might be expected to do. This theory would link the work of art to the observer's experience of it. In literary terms, it is the sort of theory which makes the reader an integral part of the poem, and so defies the injunction by Wimsatt and Beardsley against "The Affective Fallacy." Another critical theorist, Stanley Fish, has written on "The Affective Fallacy Fallacy," and more and more writers are turning to what is sometimes called "reader-response criticism." (The description of Ashbery's prosody with which I began assumes the same general theory of poetry and criticism.[6]) The climate is excellent for Ashbery's reception, and he has received wider critical acclaim than perhaps any of his contemporaries. Both his poetry and current critical theory would seem to grow from the same sources in intellectual history and to belong to the same historical and literary movement.

I want to go on to a final set of distinctions that the poem carefully manipulates. The "meaning" of a word has two aspects. Its *reference* is something nonlinguistic that the word can be said to name or point to; its *sense* is its relation to other words within the language or within a more specific linguistic context. Many words have no reference at all ("at," "which," "the," etc.), and Ashbery's emphasis on such words is consistent enough to constitute the main difficulty of reading his poetry. Pronouns provide the best example, since the reference of a pronoun is always indirect, through some antecedent. In a passage like the end of section v of "Self-Portrait" (291-310), the word *it* loses even that degree of referentiality. Its antecedent appears to be "Your argument, Francesco"; but "argument" is itself a complex metaphor, so that its reference is not plain.

> . . . Your argument, Francesco,
> Had begun to grow stale as no answer
> Or answers were forthcoming. If it dissolves now
> Into dust, that only means its time had come
> Some time ago, but look now, and listen:
> It may be that another life is stocked there
> In recesses no one knew of; that it,
> Not we, are the change; that we are in fact it

> If we could get back to it, relive some of the way
> It looked, turn our faces to the globe as it sets
> And still be coming out all right:
> Nerves normal, breath normal. Since it is a metaphor
> Made to include us, we are a part of it and
> Can live in it as in fact we have done,
> Only leaving our minds bare for questioning
> We now see will not take place at random
> But in an orderly way that means to menace
> Nobody—the normal way things are done,
> Like the concentric growing up of days
> Around a life: correctly, if you think about it.

Most simply, "argument" (and thus "it") may refer to the painting. But much that Ashbery says about "it" can have only the most indirect relation to the painting as an object ("we are in fact it/If we could get back to it"). In fact, "it" changes meaning according to context; its meaning behaves like a sense, not a reference. Yet "it" stands pronominally for "argument"; thus the "argument," the painting, carried through the passage by "it," also changes meaning with context. The referential function even of an apparently concrete term is absorbed by the contextually governed, intralinguistic operations of sense.

More exactly, the "argument" is the painting seen as a statement by the painter. As a statement, it acts linguistically, so that its meaning naturally develops more as sense than as reference. Furthermore, the painting as "argument" communicates between the painter and the viewer. What it communicates is itself, particularly as the means by which painter and viewer are united:

> . . . Since it is a metaphor
> Made to include us, we are a part of it and
> Can live in it as in fact we have done . . . (302-4)

The "us" that it includes comprises Parmigiano and Ashbery. But the painting also draws into itself all the contexts which make "us" who "we" are. Ashbery speaks of it as "a globe like ours" (89), as "life englobed" (55), as the world that is our space and whose turning defines our time. No longer simply an occasion for "reflection" on the self, it becomes also the content and structure of "reflection" itself. In short, the painting is an experience which unites the thing experienced with the one who experiences it and includes in itself the whole of his experience—of his self—for as long as he looks at it actually or in imagination. It is the model for all attentive experience, all moments made real by imagination, and its time is an eternal present, from which "what yesterday/Was like" is a distraction that arises only when "the attention/Turns dully away" (100-105).

The instruction to the poem's reader could not be more plain. Ashbery's theme invites us to participate in his poem as an experience, as he experiences the painting. To see how his method allows us to do this, and to appreciate the odds against which he manages it, is to grasp the breadth of his innovation and possibly to glimpse the new direction of contemporary poetry. To do this, we need to turn back once again to the origins of modernist poetics and examine one more distinction that Ashbery transcends.

As I discussed in the last chapter, Pound and Eliot began with the perception of a "poetic fact" that "pre-exists." For Eliot, this "fact" took the form of an "objective correlative," which, like the reference of a word, is a verbal function that points outside the linguistic context of the poem to the world of things. The poem's operation depends on this separation between words and things, which allows the poet to rejoin the two realms by mimesis. Another version of the "poetic fact" is Pound's "absolute rhythm." Within the modernist tradition, "absolute rhythm" seems merely a specialized form of the objective correlative. But unlike the latter it resides *within* the poem as language. It is the province of the third Imagist tenet, while the first two support the function of the Image as an objective correlative.

What Pound meant by the primary tenet, "Direct treatment

of the 'thing,' " is made more explicit whenever he repeats his injunction—certainly the chief rule of modernist poetic language—against abstractions. The implicit goal of the modernist poem is to become a concrete, particular experience—not discursively *about* experience. This is the purpose of the objective correlative, which in turn depends on the possibility of bringing things into the poem by means of concrete language. Yet as Robert Pinsky points out, all language is necessarily abstract; "every word is an abstraction or category, not a particular: 'foot' is no more concrete than 'trepidation' or 'cosine,' and 'large foot' or 'Robert's large foot' merely add categories" (85, 5). Understood rigorously, then, the objective correlative is an impossibility. This is to take more literally than Eliot meant it a phrase that has been immensely useful as a talisman and method. The point is that to get modernism under way, it was necessary to distort the function of poetic language in the direction of things, so as to distract it from the imposed mediation of merely personal expression. Any theory of poetry leaves some stones conveniently unturned, and modernist poets have created some of the most subtle and powerful mimetic verse ever written. But the movement away from definable, concrete situations as the basis of the poem had already begun in the *Four Quartets*, partly because of their didactic theological purpose. Eventually the logical flaw—or the mimetic separation of poetic language from experience—must fail to satisfy; and this seems to be the point from which Ashbery started.

It might appear that the inherent abstraction of language absolutely prevents poetry from attaining the goal sought by modernists, the poem as direct experience. Pinsky, indeed, goes on to complete this argument by saying that free verse—part of the modernist drive toward concreteness—must fail in that drive as thoroughly as the objective correlative: "The most basic of abstract concepts are similarity and recurrence. All forms—the repeating curve of the circle or the most subtle, free-seeming rhythm—are based on similarity, exact or slight, between particular moments" (85, 179n). But "similar-

ity" and "recurrence" are abstract terms used to describe
rhythm; they are not rhythm itself. Rhythm, like any other
concrete experience, can be thought of as based on or de-
scended from abstract principles such as recurrence; but by
that argument *no* experience can be concrete, and the term
loses significance. There is one way in which words are con-
crete things; and Olson's emphasis on the *sound* of syllables
and lines and poems is a step in Ashbery's direction. While the
concept of the objective correlative is deeply entangled in the
mimetic relation between words and things, rhythm can
claim to be direct experience. And if it is, in Pound's phrase,
an "absolute rhythm," then by definition it embodies a mean-
ing.

In "Self-Portrait," by absorbing the reference of words into
sense and by eliminating the distance between himself and his
material, Ashbery removes the mimetic function of the objec-
tive correlative from its accustomed central place in the poem.
The painting is no more objective than subjective. It does not
occupy the same position with respect to the poem as does the
mist in Levertov's, or Breughel's painting in "Musée des
Beaux Arts," or the mirror in Bogan's "The Cupola." "Self-
Portrait" resembles a modernist poem liberated—witness its
length—from objects, which in turn it liberates. It shows
none of the modernist insistence on exclusively "concrete"
language, but lets words be what—despite a glorious illu-
sion—they always were: abstract. The language is free to dis-
cuss, to explain, to move from diction to diction and, where
appropriate, to present images. Yet Ashbery has not aban-
doned the ideal of the poem as direct experience; nor does he
turn inward away from the reader. Instead, providing a model
and rationale by his own participation in Parmigiano's self-
portrait, he encourages us to join him.

This encouragement comes about in a way quite different
from the Imagist establishment of a common ground out in
the nonlinguistic world that both poet and reader inhabit. In
some important ways, that world hardly exists as far as
Ashbery's poem is concerned, and the common ground is

elsewhere. John Malcolm Brinnin, in a review that discusses Ashbery's aleatoric method of writing, again clarifies the poet's true debt to modernism, and his departure from it: "very often he reminds one of Wallace Stevens—Stevens carried one logical step further, Stevens dispossessed of his subjects. . . . As with Stevens, poetry for Ashbery is not a discrimination among units of intellectual or emotive attention but an ongoing process—'The poem of the act of the mind' " (22, 7). The prosody of "Self-Portrait in a Convex Mirror"— the continuum of events in which the reader can participate directly because they are linguistic events—is the substance of this process, which is the meaning of the poem.

Appendix

Full Texts of Three Quoted Poems

Marianne Moore: "Bird-Witted" (78d)

With innocent wide penguin eyes, three
   large fledgling mockingbirds below
the pussy-willow tree,
   stand in a row,
wings touching, feebly solemn,
till they see
    their no longer larger
    mother bringing
something which will partially
feed one of them.

Toward the high-keyed intermittent squeak
   of broken carriage springs, made by
the three similar, meek-
   coated bird's-eye
freckled forms she comes; and when
from the beak
    of one, the still living
    beetle has dropped
out, she picks it up and puts
it in again.

Standing in the shade till they have dressed
   their thickly filamented, pale
pussy-willow-surfaced
   coats, they spread tail

and wings, showing one by one,
the modest
    white stripe lengthwise on the
    tail and crosswise
underneath the wing, and the
accordion

is closed again. What delightful note
  with rapid unexpected flute
sounds leaping from the throat
  of the astute
grown bird, comes back to one from
the remote
    unenergetic sun-
    lit air before
the brood was here? How harsh
the bird's voice has become.

A piebald cat observing them,
  is slowly creeping toward the trim
trio on the tree stem.
  Unused to him
the three make room—uneasy
new problem.
    A dangling foot that missed
    its grasp, is raised
and finds the twig on which it
planned to perch. The

parent darting down, nerved by what chills
  the blood, and by hope rewarded—
of toil—since nothing fills
  squeaking unfed
mouths, wages deadly combat,
and half kills

with bayonet beak and
cruel wings, the
intellectual cautious-
ly creeping cat.

Philip Larkin: "CHURCH GOING" (67)

Once I am sure there's nothing going on
I step inside, letting the door thud shut.
Another church: matting, seats, and stone,
And little books; sprawlings of flowers, cut
For Sunday, brownish now; some brass and stuff
Up at the holy end; the small neat organ;
And a tense, musty, unignorable silence,
Brewed God knows how long. Hatless, I take off
My cycle-clips in awkward reverence,

Move forward, run my hand around the font.
From where I stand, the roof looks almost new—
Cleaned, or restored? Someone would know: I don't.
Mounting the lectern, I peruse a few
Hectoring large-scale verses, and pronounce
'Here endeth' much more loudly than I'd meant.
The echoes snigger briefly. Back at the door
I sign the book, donate an Irish sixpence,
Reflect the place was not worth stopping for.

Yet stop I did: in fact I often do,
And always end much at a loss like this,
Wondering what to look for; wondering, too,
When churches fall completely out of use
What we shall turn them into, if we shall keep
A few cathedrals chronically on show,

Their parchment, plate and pyx in locked cases,
And let the rest rent-free to rain and sheep.
Shall we avoid them as unlucky places?

Or, after dark, will dubious women come
To make their children touch a particular stone;
Pick simples for a cancer; or on some
Advised night see walking a dead one?
Power of some sort or other will go on
In games, in riddles, seemingly at random;
But superstition, like belief, must die,
And what remains when disbelief has gone?
Grass, weedy pavement, brambles, buttress, sky,

A shape less recognizable each week,
A purpose more obscure. I wonder who
Will be the last, the very last, to seek
This place for what it was; one of the crew
That tap and jot and know what rood-lofts were?
Some ruin-bibber, randy for antique,
Or Christmas-addict, counting on a whiff
Of gown-and-bands and organ-pipes and myrrh?
Or will he be my representative,

Bored, uninformed, knowing the ghostly silt
Dispersed, yet tending to this cross of ground
Through suburb scrub because it held unspilt
So long and equably what since is found
Only in separation—marriage, and birth,
And death, and thoughts of these—for whom was built
This special shell? For, though I've no idea
What this accoutred frowsty barn is worth,
It pleases me to stand in silence here;

A serious house on serious earth it is,
In whose blent air all our compulsions meet,
Are recognised, and robed as destinies.
And that much never can be obsolete,
Since someone will forever be surprising
A hunger in himself to be more serious,
And gravitating with it to this ground,
Which, he once heard, was proper to grow wise in,
If only that so many dead lie round.

John Berryman: DREAM SONG #29 (17, 33)

There sat down, once, a thing on Henry's heart
só heavy, if he had a hundred years
& more, & weeping, sleepless, in all them time
Henry could not make good.
Starts again always in Henry's ears
the little cough somewhere, an odour, a chime.

And there is another thing he has in mind
like a grave Sienese face a thousand years
would fail to blur the still profiled reproach of. Ghastly,
with open eyes, he attends, blind.
All the bells say: too late. This is not for tears;
thinking.

But never did Henry, as he thought he did,
end anyone and hacks her body up
and hide the pieces, where they may be found.
He knows: he went over everyone, & nobody's missing.
Often he reckons, in the dawn, them up.
Nobody is ever missing.

Notes

1. To avoid cluttering the book with notes, I refer to texts by the method common in scientific journals. In each reference, the first number in parentheses indicates an entry in the numbered list of references (which is intended only for this purpose and does not pretend to be a comprehensive bibliography); the number after the comma indicates the page. Multiple references are separated by semicolons.

NOTES TO CHAPTER ONE

1. Thus Robert Bridges (21, 647): "First of all it is expedient to get rid of the word Poetry. I shall not discuss the difference between poetry and prose, but merely the distinctive forms of verse and prose. The term Free Verse implies that it is with form that we have to deal, and not with content."

2. And in fact of all sound. Cf. Cary F. Jacob (55, 360): "All forms of art having the human voice as their medium of expression must depend upon four attributes of sound for their effects,—namely, pitch, tone-color, duration, and intensity."

3. I am unconvinced of the need to discriminate between "accent" and "stress" in a discussion of verse, and will use the two interchangeably. For the exacting reader, the entries under the two words in the *Princeton Encyclopedia of Poetry and Poetics* may be of interest.

4. Insufficient attention to the relation between stress and meaning limits the otherwise fascinating study, *English Stress*, by Morris Halle and Samuel Keyser. The flaw first becomes evident when they discuss, in passing, stress in phrases rather than single words (44, 15-29). The same constriction in their linguistic focus imposes a much more serious limitation on their theory of meter. A fundamental thesis of my book is that prosody both determines and derives from meaning; for this reason, I will rarely refer to Halle and Keyser even in my remarks on metrical verse.

5. Mr. Kenner has warned me in conversation that, in the heat of revision, Moore sometimes forgot to preserve the syllabic patterns

she had established. It is true that earlier printed versions of the poem are entirely regular. (For the whole story, see the List of Reference entries under Marianne Moore.) The nature of the revision indicates that the consecutive anomalies may well be accidental; they result from a single alteration. Whether or not this fact (with a deduction from it about Moore's intention, or lack of it) invalidates my interpretation raises intricate and fascinating problems of critical theory. Here I would note only that the anomalies are strikingly appropriate, and their effect is entirely in accord with the spirit of the poem as Mr. Kenner has so lucidly analyzed it.

6. Several systems of scansion are or have been in use. Musical scansion will be discussed in Chapter Two. I use the system that seems simplest to me, since scansion cannot reasonably pretend to exactitude in showing even the accentual element in rhythm. My marks for accent, caesura, and secondary accent are the most common ones. I substitute an × for the breve ($\cup$) often used for slack syllables. Though our system of scansion derives from that of Latin, the elements scanned are different; we recognize this by replacing the macron ($-$) with the accent, and it seems more consistent and less confusing to do the same with slack syllables, which are not the same as short ones. In general I follow the scansion practices of (for instance) Brooks and Warren (23), though I rarely see any need for their "hovering accent," preferring to believe that English metrical practice includes the spondee.

7. Other writers, on both sides, were more careful: Llewellyn Jones (57, 395) notes that some upholders of free verse "misrepresent" metered verse "by confounding its metre and its rhythm, which latter is a free movement emphasized and made more measureable to the ear by being written against a metric scheme." Mary Hall Leonard (68, 30) remarks that one of the difficulties of scansion is that "prosodists themselves are often hazy as to whether they are considering the conventional feet of the verse *patterns*, or the variations embroidered on the pattern by overweight and underweight in the syllables of the foot itself." Finally, Amy Lowell seems to half-understand the matter when, in "Poetry as a Spoken Art"—to which H. E. Warner's article of the same name is a reply—she says that the fact that free verse "may dispense with rhyme, and must dispense with metre, does not affect its substance in the least. For no matter with what it dispenses, it retains that essential to all poetry: Rhythm" (71, 49).

8. "Tension" is used by Wimsatt and Beardsley (though they later come to "interplay"), and by most New Critics. Yvor Winters uses "counterpoint," but in a rather different way. He shrewdly suggests, however, that accentual-syllabic verse is inherently counterpointed (109). One might go on to speculate that some kind of counterpoint is essential to the success of any verse. A. D. Hope claims that it is (50, 41-43), as do other writers trying to prove that verse needs meter. But though meter may use or create counterpoint, they are not the same thing, at least by my definition. Here, "counterpoint" will refer, not to the inevitable (and metrically fundamental) interplay between actual and abstract rhythmic patterns, but to the relation between equally actual systems. The question—which I will tackle in Chapter Four—is whether counterpoint as a mode of organization is a sufficient framework to sustain a prosody.

Notes to Chapter Two

1. Kenneth Pike, in *The Intonation of American English*, implies the broader technical reason for calling quantitative verse impossible in English (84, 34): The quantity of a syllable is variable, depending on the number of syllables with which it is grouped between stresses, because the stresses themselves tend to be distributed equally in time—a fact that will be important in the third part of this chapter. Thus quantity in English syllables is contextually governed and not available for *separate* manipulation, as a metrical element must be.

2. Emma Mellard Kafalenos, *Possibilities of Isochrony*, Diss. Washington University, 1974. Like other theorists examined in the last part of this chapter, Kafalenos succumbs to the temptation to claim that her system accounts for all free verse. Her work remains, however, one of the best to date on Williams's late prosody.

3. This follows, in ways it would be beside my point to explore in detail, from both the theories of Wimsatt and Beardsley and those of Jespersen and Chatman with which they quarrel (108, 593).

4. Lanier also uses the notation badly. Unlike Hopkins, he is oblivious to the idea of anacrusis, which would match the stressed notes with the beginnings of measures:

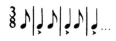

If one reverses the argument and takes the scansion as prosodic—as embodying not a performance but directions for one—the result is strikingly unnatural. The experiment is worth trying. Saintsbury's remarks on Lanier (and on Omond) are also well worth examining (92, III, 493-97).

NOTES TO CHAPTER THREE

1. There is a fourth term, speech, of which I want to dispose quickly. When Molière's Philosophy Master reveals to M. Jourdain that all his life the Bourgeois Gentilhomme has been speaking prose, he muddies a distinction Aristotle would have insisted on. Art imitates nature. As Northrop Frye puts it, art creates "a form of which nature is the content" (40, 164). The artist may imitate nature more or less closely, for various purposes; but the most "accurate" painting of a mountain is not a mountain. A novel and a poem both imitate speech; neither one *is* speech. What I say in this chapter about poetry, verse and prose—all of which inhabit the realm of mimesis—has some bearing on *how* they perform the imitation; and my last chapters add occasional considerations of these relationships. But their details are material for a separate study.

2. This statement, on which a great deal I will say hereafter is founded, is remarkably hard to prove. Surely one reader pauses where another rushes on, and demonstration would soon entail the "performative fallacy." But again, as with similar matters in the first chapter, I am less interested in acoustic than in psychological facts. If a reader feels nothing at the end of a line—no suspense, no tension between closure and continuity, no momentary hitch—it is hard to imagine any use at all for lineation, whether in metrical or nonmetrical verse.

3. The considerations that follow overlap the subject of enjambement, which occupies most of the next chapter. John Hollander gives an excellent account of enjambement in metrical verse in "The Sense Variously Drawn Out," *Vision and Resonance* (48).

NOTES TO CHAPTER FIVE

1. Aristotle completes the circle by identifying formal cause—essential nature, or meaning—as final cause: "Also, since the term 'nature' is applied both to material and to form, and since it is the

latter that constitutes the goal, and all else is for the sake of that goal, it follows that the form is the final cause" (*Physics*, II. viii).

2. In conversation. A version of the dictum appears in his essay, "Speaking Silence": "A poem is not so much a thought, or series of thoughts, as it is a mind" (80, 103).

3. "The form is mechanic, when on any given material we impress a pre-determined form, not necessarily arising out of the properties of the material;—as when to a mass of wet clay we give whatever shape we wish it to retain when hardened. The organic form, on the other hand, is innate; it shapes, as it develops, itself from within, and the fulness of its development is one and the same with the perfection of its outward form. Such as the life is, such is the form" (28, 432-33). Owen Barfield points out that Coleridge would not have defended an opposition between living and inanimate objects (13, 44). Partly because of this implied opposition, however—the virtuous plant against the inhuman machine—"organic form" has often been taken up as a revolutionary slogan. Hence its decay into a vague laudatory phrase. Walter Sutton, who points out Emerson's role in the development of "organicism" in America, uses the phrase this way. Generally, Sutton wishes to "identify certain tendencies in Romantic poetic theory and practice that have special importance for the modern revolution in poetry. Among these was the abandonment of neoclassical fixed forms (like the heroic couplet) and genre distinctions in favor of organically determined functional forms" (98, 4). This is essentially correct, and I will summarize this prosodic history later in this chapter. But it is important to note that Coleridge presented his definition not as a program for reform but as a way of reading the great poetry of the past, specifically Shakespeare's.

4. The result is clear in Wimsatt's "Organic Form" (107). He argues—as Coleridge would not (13, 125)—that organicism is merely a metaphor, and condemns any but the most general use of the term. So complete is his reduction of the idea that his motive in retaining it at all is unclear.

5. On Romantic "sincerity," see David Perkins (83, especially Chapter One). Lionel Trilling's *Sincerity and Authenticity* (101) is also helpful, especially in pointing out that the opposition to machines sometimes implied by "organicism" was sharply qualified at around the time when free verse was beginning.

6. I will discuss the relation of free verse to modernist poetics in greater detail in my seventh chapter.

7. Though these issues call for a chapter of their own—my seventh—it might be helpful to present here the context of Pound's phrase, since it bears on what follows: "I believe in an 'absolute rhythm,' a rhythm, that is, in poetry which corresponds exactly to the emotion or shade of emotion to be expressed. A man's rhythm must be interpretative, it will be, therefore, in the end, his own, un-counterfeiting, uncounterfeitable" (87, 9).

8. It is possible to read the poem differently, by calling it a dramatic monologue and assuming that the speaker is someone distinctly other than the poet—someone whose gossip he has overheard. But the structure of meaning, established so much more strongly by form (especially lineation) than by what is actually said, would change little. I have chosen to assume that the poet and speaker are (as much as they ever can be) one, because it simplifies the terms of the analysis. But in any case, though we might assign the *saying* to another speaker, we would still feel the poem's *meaning* as being discovered in that saying by the poet who controls its prosodic organization.

Notes to Chapter Six

1. The lines all pass the tests for metricality established by Halle and Keyser in their linguistic theory of meter (44, 169-71). But their system of scansion would make the last syllable of "organ" extrametrical, as though it were part of a feminine rhyme—which it is not. I will comment again briefly on their system in the third section of this chapter.

2. Gardner recognized her own analysis as tentative, and offered a warning: "In this matter of metre the poets go before and the prosodists follow after, often a very long time after. What 'rules' prosodists of the future will discover that Mr Eliot has in practice obeyed I do not know. If I were to try to formulate any now I should almost certainly be proved wrong by whatever verse he writes next" (42, 16).

3. Allen's analysis should make clear, if it is not sufficiently clear to begin with, that Whitman's techniques will not provide an adequate model for most modern free verse. Benjamin Hrushovski's prolegomena to any future prosodic theory of "Free Rhythms in Modern Poetry" (54) covertly assumes Whitman as such a model, and consequently reaches a dead-end.

NOTES TO CHAPTER SEVEN

1. I take much of what follows from my own treatment of the same questions—in somewhat expanded form and with a different focus—in "Condensation: The Critical Vocabulary of Pound and Eliot" (46).

2. "Imitates" in an Aristotelian more than a Platonic sense—though the preexistence of the "poetic fact" certainly has Platonic overtones. Here as elsewhere (I have quoted it before) I mean to suggest a definition of mimesis like Northrop Frye's: Art imitates nature by "creating a form of which nature is the content" (40, 164). This definition allies mimesis with (proportional) metaphor in ways I hinted at in Chapter Five.

3. In the last analysis, Mizener may be correct. My argument here concerns the critical concepts of Pound and Eliot as they must be understood within the modernist frame of reference. When we turn to more contemporary poetry in the next chapter, some of the same concepts will necessarily change in relative value and even in meaning.

4. Again, there is less than meets the eye in this distinction. What Eliot rejects is only the equation of poetry with "the spontaneous overflow of powerful feeling"—which Wordsworth himself qualifies with the strikingly Yeatsian formulation, "emotion recollected in tranquility." Eliot condemns this phrase, too; but his argument depends notably on nit-picking (35, 43).

NOTES TO CHAPTER EIGHT

1. There are important exceptions. Both John Berryman and John Ashbery, whom we will examine later, seem to have learned their chief prosodic lessons from Eliot, and not simply from the metrical tradition he partly represented.

2. As Howard Nemerov has it, "The poet's task has generally been conceded to be hard, but it may be so described as to make it logically impossible: Make an object recognizable as an individual of the class p for poem, but make it in such a way that it resembles no other individual of that class" (80, 130).

3. Olson hints also at a further distinction, between the poem as object and as referential language, which as we shall see takes on a new significance for a poet like Ashbery.

4. In quotations from Berryman, the parenthetical numbers do not refer to my List of References—all quotations are from (17)—but to the numbered poems in *The Dream Songs*.

5. The poem comes from the collection of the same name (8). For reference in the text, I will give line numbers; but since these do not appear in the published poem, here is a summary of lengths for sections (also unnumbered, but clearly identifiable as verse paragraphs): I, lines 1-99; II, 100-150; III, 151-206; IV, 207-50; V, 251-310; VI, 311-552.

6. Such a theory is, in M. H. Abrams's terms (1), a "pragmatic" one, not "expressive" like Romantic poetic theory, nor "mimetic" like the modernism of Pound and Eliot, nor "objective" like the New Criticism.

List of References

1. Abrams, M. H. *The Mirror and the Lamp: Romantic Theory and the Critical Tradition*. 1953; rpt. New York: Norton, 1958.
2. Aiken, Conrad. "The Function of Rhythm." *Dial*, 65 (Nov. 16, 1918), 417-18.
3. Aldington, Richard. "Free Verse in England." *Egoist*, 1 (Sept. 15, 1914), 351-52.
4. Allen, Donald M., ed. *The New American Poetry*. New York: Grove, 1960.
5. Allen, Gay Wilson. *American Prosody*. American Literature Series. New York: American Book Company, 1935.
6. Andrews, C. E. "The Rhythm of Prose and of Free Verse." *Sewanee Review*, 26 (Apr. 1918), 183-94.
7. Aristotle. *Physics*. Trans. Philip H. Wicksteed and Francis M. Cornford. Loeb ed. London: William Heinemann, 1929.
8. Ashbery, John. "Self-Portrait in a Convex Mirror" (poem). *Self-Portrait in a Convex Mirror*. New York: Viking, 1975, pp. 68-83.
9. Auden, W[ystan] H[ugh]. "Musée des Beaux Arts" (poem). *Collected Poems*. New York: Random House, 1976, pp. 146-47.
10. Baker, William E. *Syntax in English Poetry: 1870-1930*. Berkeley: Univ. of California Press, 1967.
11. Baldwin, Summerfield. "Two Unessentials of Poetry." *Poetry Review of America*, 2 (Feb. 1917), 60-61.
12. Barfield, Owen. "Poetry, Verse and Prose." *New Statesman*, 31 (Oct. 6, 1928), 793-94.
13. ———. *What Coleridge Thought*. Middletown, Conn.: Wesleyan Univ. Press, 1971.
14. Barry, Sister M. Martin, O. P. *An Analysis of the Prosodic Structure of Selected Poems of T. S. Eliot*. Revised ed. Washington, D.C.: Catholic Univ. of America Press, 1969.
15. Baum, Paull F. "Sprung Rhythm." *PMLA*, 74 (Sept. 1959), 418-25.
16. Beckett, Lucy. *Wallace Stevens*. London: Cambridge Univ. Press, 1974.

17. Berryman, John. *The Dream Songs.* New York: Farrar, Straus & Giroux, 1969.
18. Bogan, Louise. "The Cupola" (poem). *The Blue Estuaries: Poems 1923-1968.* American Poetry Series. New York: The Ecco Press, 1977.
19. Boomslitter, Paul C., Warren Creel, and George S. Hastings, Jr. "Perception and English Poetic Meter." *PMLA,* 88 (Mar. 1973), 200-208.
20. Bradley, Sculley. "The Fundamental Metrical Principle in Whitman's Poetry." *American Literature,* 10 (Mar. 1938-Jan. 1939), 437-59.
21. Bridges, Robert. "A Paper on Free Verse." *North American Review,* 216 (Nov. 1922), 647-58.
22. Brinnin, John Malcolm. "Self-Portrait in a Convex Mirror" (review). *The New York Times Book Review,* Aug. 10, 1975, pp. 7-8.
23. Brooks, Cleanth, and Robert Penn Warren. *Understanding Poetry.* Third ed. New York: Holt, Rinehart, 1960.
24. Burroughs, John. "The Reds of American Literature." *Current Opinion,* 70 (Apr. 1921), 550-51.
25. Christy, Arthur E. "Chinoiserie and Vers Libre." *Open Court,* 43 (Apr. 1929), 209-18.
26. Coleridge, Samuel Taylor. *Biographia Literaria.* Ed. J. Shawcross. 2 vols. London: Oxford Univ. Press, 1907.
27. ———. "Christabel" (poem). *Selected Poetry and Prose of Samuel Taylor Coleridge.* Ed. Donald A. Stauffer. New York: Random House, 1951, pp. 24-43.
28. ———. "Shakespeare's Judgment Equal to His Genius." *Selected Poetry and Prose of Samuel Taylor Coleridge.* Ed. Donald A. Stauffer. New York: Random House, 1951, pp. 429-33.
29. Cone, Eddie Gay. *The Free-Verse Controversy in American Magazines: 1912-1922.* Diss. Duke Univ. 1971.
30. Cunningham, J. V. "How Shall the Poem Be Written?" *The Collected Essays of J. V. Cunningham.* Chicago: Swallow Press, 1976, pp. 256-71.
31. Davie, Donald. *Articulate Energy: An Inquiry into the Syntax of English Poetry.* 1955; rpt. London: Routledge & Kegan Paul, 1976.
32. Eliot, T[homas] S[tearns]. "The Borderline of Prose." *New Statesman,* 9 (May 19, 1917), 157-59.

33. ———. *Collected Poems: 1909-1962*. New York: Harcourt, Brace, 1963.

34. ———. *Ezra Pound: His Metric and Poetry*. New York: Knopf, 1917. Rpt. in *To Criticize the Critic*. New York: Farrar, Straus, 1965, pp. 162-82.

35. ———. *Selected Prose of T. S. Eliot*. Ed. Frank Kermode. New York: Harcourt Brace Jovanovich and Farrar, Straus & Giroux, 1975.

36. Ficke, Arthur Davison. "Metrical Freedom and the Contemporary Poet." *Dial*, 58 (Jan. 1, 1915), 11-13.

37. Fletcher, John Gould. "A Rational Explanation of Vers Libre." *Dial*, 66 (Jan. 11, 1919), 11-13.

38. Flint, F. S. Preface to *Otherworld* (first book of poems, 1920). Quoted by Glenn Y. Hughes, *Imagism and the Imagists*. Stanford: Stanford Univ. Press, 1931, p. 78.

39. Frye, Northrop. *Anatomy of Criticism: Four Essays*. 1957; rpt. New York: Atheneum, 1968.

40. ———. "The Realistic Oriole: A Study of Wallace Stevens." In *Wallace Stevens: A Collection of Critical Essays*. Twentieth-Century Views. Ed. Marie Borroff. Englewood Cliffs, N.J.: Prentice-Hall, 1963, pp. 161-76.

41. Fuller, Henry B. "A New Field for Free Verse." *Dial*, 61 (Dec. 14, 1916), 515-17.

42. Gardner, Helen. *The Art of T. S. Eliot*. 1950; rpt. New York: Dutton, 1959.

43. Gross, Harvey. *Sound and Form in Modern Poetry*. Ann Arbor: Univ. of Michigan Press, 1964.

44. Halle, Morris, and Samuel J. Keyser. *English Stress: Its Form, Its Growth, and Its Role in Verse*. New York: Harper & Row, 1971.

45. Hartman, Charles O. "Analysis of a Song: Joni Mitchell's 'Michael from Mountains.' " *Centennial Review*, 21 (fall 1977), 401-13.

46. ———. "Condensation: The Critical Vocabulary of Pound and Eliot." *College English*, 39 (Oct. 1977), 179-90.

47. ———. "The Criticism of Song." *Centennial Review*, 19 (spring 1975), 96-107.

48. Hollander, John. *Vision and Resonance: Two Senses of Poetic Form*. New York: Oxford Univ. Press, 1975.

49. Hooker, Brian. "The Rhythmic Relation of Prose and Verse." *Forum*, 41 (Apr. 1909), 424-37.

50. Hope, A[lec] D[erwent]. *The Cave and the Spring.* 1965; rpt. Chicago: Univ. of Chicago Press, 1970.

51. ―――. Quoted, from a 1963 preface, in *Norton Anthology of Modern Poetry.* Ed. Richard Ellmann and Robert O'Clair. New York: Norton, 1973, p. 766.

52. Hopkins, Gerard Manley. "The Windhover" (poem). *Norton Anthology of Modern Poetry.* Ed. Richard Ellmann and Robert O'Clair. New York: Norton, 1973, p. 81.

53. Hough, Graham. *Image and Experience: Reflections on a Literary Revolution.* Lincoln, Neb.: Univ. of Nebraska Press, 1960.

54. Hrushovski, Benjamin. "On Free Rhythms in Modern Poetry: Preliminary Remarks toward a Critical Theory of Their Structures and Functions." In *Style in Language.* Ed. Thomas A. Sebeok. Cambridge, Mass.: M.I.T. Press, 1960, pp. 173–90.

55. Jacob, Cary F. "Rhythm in Prose and in Poetry." *Quarterly Journal of Speech Education,* 13 (Nov. 1927), 357–75.

56. Johnson, Burges. *New Rhyming Dictionary and Poets' Handbook.* New York: Harper, 1931.

57. Jones, Llewellyn. "Free Verse and Its Propaganda." *Sewanee Review,* 28 (July 1920), 384–95.

58. Kafalenos, Emma Mellard. *Possibilities of Isochrony.* Diss. Washington Univ., 1974.

59. Keats, John. Letter to John Taylor, 27 February 1818. In *Selected Poems and Letters.* Ed. Douglas Bush. Boston: Houghton Mifflin, 1959, p. 267.

60. Kenner, Hugh. *A Homemade World: The American Modernist Writers.* New York: William Morrow, 1975.

61. ―――. *The Invisible Poet: T. S. Eliot.* New York: McDowell, Obolensky, 1959.

62. ―――. "Meditation and Enactment." In *Marianne Moore: A Collection of Critical Essays.* Twentieth-Century Views. Ed. Charles Tomlinson. Englewood Cliffs, N.J.: Prentice-Hall, 1969, pp. 159–64.

63. ―――. *The Poetry of Ezra Pound.* London: Faber & Faber, 1951.

64. Kessler, Edward. *Images of Wallace Stevens.* New Brunswick, N.J.: Rutgers Univ. Press, 1972.

65. Kilmer, Joyce. "How Does the New Poetry Differ from the Old?" (interview of Amy Lowell). *New York Times Magazine,* March 26, 1916, p. 8.

66. Kramer, Hilton. "A Sanctuary for Outsiders" (review of *The Lit-*

tle Magazine in America). New York Times Book Review, Feb. 4, 1979, pp. 9-32.

67. Larkin, Philip. "Church Going" (poem). *The Less Deceived.* (Marvell Press, 1952). Rpt. in *Norton Anthology of Modern Poetry.* Ed. Richard Ellmann and Robert O'Clair. New York: Norton, 1973, pp. 1015-16.

68. Leonard, Mary Hall. "A Problem in Prosody." *Poetry Journal*, 7 (Apr. 1917), 14-30.

69. Levertov, Denise. "The Ground-Mist" (poem). *O Taste and See.* New York: New Directions, 1964, p. 40.

70. Lowell, Amy. "A Consideration of Modern Poetry." *North American Review*, 205 (Jan. 1917), 103-17.

71. ———. "Poetry as a Spoken Art." *Dial*, 62 (Jan. 25, 1917), 46-49.

72. ———. "The Rhythms of Free Verse." *Dial*, 64 (Jan. 17, 1918), 51-56.

73. ———. "Some Musical Analogies in Modern Poetry." *Musical Quarterly*, 6 (Jan. 1920), 127-57.

74. ———. "Vers Libre and Metrical Prose." *Poetry*, 3 (Mar. 1914), 213-20.

75. Milton, John. *Complete Poems and Major Prose.* Ed. Merrit Y. Hughes. New York: Odyssey, 1957.

76. Mizener, Arthur. "To Meet Mr. Eliot." In *T. S. Eliot: A Collection of Critical Essays.* Twentieth-Century Views. Ed. Hugh Kenner. Englewood Cliffs, N.J.: Prentice-Hall, 1962, pp. 15-27.

77. Monroe, Harriet. "Rhythms of English Verse." *Poetry*, 3 (Nov. 1913), 61-68; 3 (Dec. 1913), 100-111.

78. Moore, Marianne. "Bird-Witted" (poem). (a) *New Republic*, 85 (Jan. 22, 1936), 311. (b) *What Are Years?* New York: Macmillan, 1941, pp. 22-24. (c) *Collected Poems.* New York: Macmillan, 1951, pp. 106-8. (d) *Complete Poems.* New York: Macmillan, 1967, pp. 105-6.

79. Morris, John N. "Summer School" (poem). *The Life Beside This One.* New York: Atheneum, 1975, p. 25.

80. Nemerov, Howard. *Figures of Thought.* Boston: David Godine, 1978.

81. O[mond], T. S. "The Limits of Verse-Length." *Living Age*, 258 (July 11, 1908), 119-22.

82. Oppenheim, James. " 'Lazy' Verse." *Seven Arts*, 1 (Nov. 1916), 66-72.

83. Perkins, David. *Wordsworth and the Poetry of Sincerity*. Cambridge: Harvard Univ. Press, Belknap Press, 1964.

84. Pike, Kenneth L. *The Intonation of American English*. University of Michigan Publications: Linguistics I. Ann Arbor: Univ. of Michigan Press, 1956.

85. Pinsky, Robert. *The Situation of Poetry: Contemporary Poetry and Its Traditions*. Princeton: Princeton Univ. Press, 1976.

86. Pound, Ezra. *ABC of Reading*. 1934; rpt. New York: New Directions, 1960.

87. ———. *Literary Essays*. Ed. T. S. Eliot. 1935; rpt. New York: New Directions, 1968.

88. *Princeton Encyclopedia of Poetry and Poetics*. Ed. Alex Preminger et al. Enlarged ed. Princeton: Princeton Univ. Press, 1974.

89. Reed, Henry. "Chard Whitlow" (poem). *The Fireside Book of Humorous Verse*. Ed. William Cole. New York: Simon & Schuster, 1959, p. 252.

90. Riddel, Joseph N. *The Clairvoyant Eye: The Poetry and Poetics of Wallace Stevens*. Baton Rouge: Louisiana State Univ. Press, 1965.

91. Saintsbury, George. *A History of English Prose Rhythm*. London: Macmillan, 1912.

92. ———. *History of English Prosody from the Twelfth Century to the Present Day*. 3 vols. London: Macmillan, 1906–10.

93. Shapiro, Karl. "English Prosody and Modern Poetry." *ELH*, 14 (June 1947), 77–92.

94. Simons, Hi. "The Genre of Wallace Stevens." In *Wallace Stevens: A Collection of Critical Essays*. Twentieth-Century Views. Ed. Marie Borroff. Englewood Cliffs, N.J.: Prentice-Hall, 1963, pp. 43–53.

95. Solt, Mary Ellen. "William Carlos Williams: Idiom and Structure." *Massachusetts Review*, 3 (winter 1962), 304–18.

96. Stevens, Wallace. "Valley Candle" (poem). *Collected Poems*. New York: Knopf, 1968, p. 51.

97. Storer, Edward. "Form in Free Verse." *New Republic*, 6 (Mar. 11, 1916), 154–56.

98. Sutton, Walter. *American Free Verse*. New York: New Directions, 1973.

99. ———. "A Conversation with Denise Levertov." *Minnesota Review*, 5 (Aug.-Oct. 1965), 322–38.

100. Thompson, John. *The Founding of English Metre*. New York: Columbia Univ. Press, 1961.

101. Trilling, Lionel. *Sincerity and Authenticity*. Cambridge: Harvard Univ. Press, 1972.

102. Warner, H. E. "Poetry and Other Things." *Dial*, 61 (Aug. 15, 1916), 91-94.

103. ———. "Poetry as a Spoken Art." *Dial*, 62 (May 3, 1917), 386.

104. Williams, William Carlos. *Paterson*. New York: New Directions, 1963.

105. ———. *Pictures from Breughel and Other Poems: Collected Poems 1950-1962*. New York: New Directions, 1962.

106. ———. *Selected Poems*. Enlarged ed. New York: New Directions, 1968.

107. Wimsatt, W. K., Jr. "Organic Form." *The Day of the Leopards*. New Haven, Conn.: Yale Univ. Press, 1976, pp. 205-23.

108. Wimsatt, W. K., Jr., and Monroe C. Beardsley. "The Concept of Meter: An Exercise in Abstraction." *PMLA*, 74 (Dec. 1959), 585-98.

109. Winters, Yvor. "Mr. Winter's [sic] Metrics." *Saturday Review of Literature*, 7 (Oct. 4, 1930), 188.

110. ———. *Primitivism and Decadence*. 1937; rpt. New York: Haskell House, 1969.

Index

Abrams, M. H., 186
absolute rhythm, 91, 93, 134-35, 168-70, 184
accent, nature of, 16-17, 54-56, 179; in accentual-syllabic verse, 21-23, 27, 70, 108, 111, 180; in English, 30, 44, 95, 114-17; in free verse, 25, 47, 65, 76, 83, 92, 96, 126. *See also* accentual meter, antithesis, isochrony
accentual meter, 88, 90, 137, 162; seen in free verse, 29-44, 64, 115-17. *See also* Anglo-Saxon prosody
accentualism, prosodic theory opposed to quantity, 4, 37, 45
accentual-syllabic meter, 16-17, 20-32, 34, 39, 41, 64, 68, 71, 87-89, 91, 116-17, 137, 181. *See also* iambic pentameter, foot, metrical substitution
affective fallacy, 166
Aiken, Conrad, 23, 46, 51
Aldington, Richard, 47, 49, 70, 92, 114-15, 130
Allen, Gay Wilson, 7, 89, 122, 184
American idiom, 96, 103-105, 137, 143, 146, 148, 156. *See also* speech
American poetry as opposed to British, 5, 103-105, 137-38
Anderson, Elliott, 145
Andrews, C. E., 53-55, 73-74
Anglo-Saxon prosody, 5, 16-17, 29-33, 35-36. *See also* accentual meter
antithesis, effect on accent, 54, 56, 77-78, 119n
Aristotle, 81, 132, 182, 183, 185
Arnold, Matthew, 70, 111, 117

Ashbery, John, 159-71, 185
Auden, W. H., 74-80, 93, 100, 121, 144, 170
auditory imagination, 134-35
authenticity, 93, 147-48; and organic form, 87-88, 183; in free verse, 27, 46, 103-105, 134-36, 154; in metrical verse, 134-36, 156-58

Baker, William E., 152
Baldwin, Summerfield, 115
Barfield, Owen, 22, 50-51, 53, 183
Barry, Sister M. Martin, 116-17
Beardsley, Monroe C., *see* Wimsatt
Bentham, Jeremy, 11
Berryman, John, 155-59, 160, 163, 177, 185, 186
Bible, 53-56, 90, 122, 136
Binyon, Laurence, 70
Blake, William, 7, 29, 48, 70, 88, 90
Bloom, Harold, 165
Bogan, Louise, 61-63, 74, 170
Booth, Wayne, 86
Bradley, Sculley, 72-74
Breughel, Pieter, 63-66, 75-80, 170
breve, *see* macrons and breves
Bridges, Robert, 5, 34, 48-49, 52, 72-73, 90, 179
Brinnin, John Malcolm, 171
Brooks, Cleanth, and Robert Penn Warren, 74, 180
Browning, Robert, 22, 88, 108, 116, 137, 139
Byron, Lord, 88, 90

cadence, 40, 46-47, 50, 92, 104, 146
caesura, 22, 56-57, 61, 72, 107, 125, 180